The Internet
Made Simple

Made Simple *Computer Books*

● easy to follow ● jargon free ● practical ● task based ● easy steps

Thousands of people have already discovered that the MADE SIMPLE series gives them what they want *fast!* These are the books for you if you want to learn quickly what's essential and how to do things with a particular piece of software. Many delighted readers have written, telephoned and e-mailed us about the Made Simple Series of Computer books. Comments have included:

● "Clear, concise and well laid out"
● "Ideal for the first time user."
● "Clear, accurate, well presented, jargon free, well targeted."
● "Easy to follow to perform a task."
● "I haven't found any other books worth recommending until these."

This best selling series is in your local bookshop now, or in case of difficulty, contact:

Heinemann Publishers, Oxford, P.O.Box 381,Oxford OX2 8EJ.
Tel 01865 314300. Fax 01865 314091. Credit card sales 01865 314627.

Series titles:

Excel for Windows	Stephen Morris	0 7506 2070 6
Lotus 1-2-3 (DOS)	Ian Robertson	0 7506 2066 8
MS-DOS	Ian Sinclair	0 7506 2069 2
MS-Works for Windows	P. K. McBride	0 7506 2065 X
Windows 3.1	P. K. McBride	0 7506 2072 2
Word for Windows	Keith Brindley	0 7506 2071 4
WordPerfect (DOS)	Stephen Copestake	0 7506 2068 4
Access for Windows	Moira Stephen	0 7506 2309 8
The Internet	P.K.McBride	0 7506 2311 X
Quicken for Windows	Stephen Copestake	0 7506 2308 X
WordPerfect for Windows	Keith Brindley	0 7506 2310 1
Lotus 123 (5.0) for Windows	Stephen Morris	0 7506 2307 1
Multimedia	Simon Collin	0 7506 2314 4
Pageplus for Windows	Ian Sinclair	0 7506 2312 8
Powerpoint	Moira Stephen	0 7506 2420 5
Hard Drives	Ian Robertson	0 7506 2313 6
Windows 95	P.K. McBride	0 7506 2306 3
WordPro	Moira Stephen	0 7506 2626 7
Office 95	P.K. McBride	0 7506 2625 9
The Internet for Windows 95	P.K.McBride	0 7506 2835 9
Word for Windows 95	Keith Brindley	0 7506 2815 4
Excel for Windows 95	Stephen Morris	0 7506 2816 2
Internet Resources	P.K.McBride	0 7506 2836 7
Powerpoint for Windows 95	Moira Stephen	0 7506 2817 0
Microsoft Networking	P.K.McBride	0 7506 2837 5
Designing Internet Home Pages	Lilian Hobbs	0 7506 2941 X
Access for Windows 95	Moira Stephen	0 7506 2818 9

The Internet
Made Simple

P.K.McBride

MADE SIMPLE
BOOKS

Made Simple
An imprint of Butterworth-Heinemann
Linacre House, Jordan Hill, Oxford OX2 8DP
A division of Reed Educational and Professional Publishing Ltd

Ⓡ   A member of the Reed Elsevier plc group

OXFORD   BOSTON   JOHANNESBURG
MELBOURNE   NEW DELHI   SINGAPORE

First published 1995
Reprinted 1995 (twice)
Revised and reprinted 1996

TRADEMARKS/REGISTERED TRADEMARKS
Computer hardware and software brand names mentioned in this book are protected
by their respective trademarks and are acknowledged.

British Library Cataloguing in Publication Data
A catalogue record for this book is available from the British Library

ISBN 0 7506 2311 X

Typeset by P.K.McBride, Southampton

Archtype, Bash Casual, Cotswold and Gravity fonts from Advanced Graphics Ltd
Icons designed by Sarah Ward © 1994
Printed and bound in Great Britain

Contents

Preface IX

1 Internet FAQs   **1**

What is it? 2
Who's on-line? 3
What's in it for me? 4
How did it start? 5
How big?! 6
How do I find people? 8
Summary 10

2 Internet services   **11**

Electronic mail 12
News 14
Netiquette 16
File transfer 18
Finding files 20
The World Wide Web 22
Gopher 24
Other services 26
Summary 28

3 Basic communications   **29**

Hardware 30
Serial ports 33
Parity and other bits 34
Data transfer protocols 36
Terminal emulation 38

Software 40

Modem commands 42

Summary 44

4 Windows Terminal — 45

The Screen 46

Settings 48

Capturing text............................... 52

Sending text files 54

Binary file transfers 56

Terminal files.............................. 58

The phone connection 59

Summary....................................... 60

5 Compuserve — 61

Making the connection 62

Getting CIM................................... 64

Setting up 66

Local nodes 68

Using WinCIM.................................. 70

Forums 72

File finder.................................... 74

Go ftp 76

Communications 78

Other services............................... 81

Summary....................................... 82

6	**WinNET**	**83**
	Starting with WinNET	84
	Setting up	86
	Off-line mail	88
	WinNET tools	90
	Newsgroup subscription	92
	The news desk	94
	Summary	96

7	**Trumpet Winsock**	**97**
	Local links to the World	98
	Trumpet Winsock	99
	Getting on-line	101
	Archie file locator	102
	ftp the easy way	104
	Gopher it	106
	Eudora mail	108
	Summary	110

8	**The World Wide Web**	**111**
	Netscape	112
	Netscape options	114
	Net Directories	116
	WWW URL's	118
	Bookmarks	120
	Hypertext	122
	Summary	124

9 Files by mail 125

Archie by mail 126
ftp by mail 128
Binaries by mail 130
Gopher by mail 132
Summary 134

10 Sources 135

UK service providers 136
Recommended ftps 140
Major ftp sites 142
Archie servers 143
Gopher servers 144

Index 145

Preface

The Internet is vast, varied and changing fast. Some parts of it are designed for very specialist audiences, some of its facilities are complex to use. Other parts are of general interest and some services are simple to access. This book concentrates on the easiest aspects, and those that will be of interest to most people – electronic mail, newsgroups, downloading files and browsing the World Wide Web.

The best way to get to grips with the Internet is to explore it. But exploration, Livingstone-style, can take you into a lot of dead ends, or round in circles. While this is fascinating, it can also be frustrating – I speak from experience. This book aims to provide you with a map, and some of the basic tools that you need, so that you don't get (too) lost.

The first four sections cover the preparations to be made while still at the base camp. They provide a crash course in the native language of the Internet, its key concepts and jargon, and look at the equipment that you will need for your expedition.

The next three sections start you off down alternative routes into the Internet, through Compuserve and the IBM PC User Group, two nationwide service providers in the UK, and through Total Connectivity Providers, a firm that is local to me, but a model of good practice.

The final sections explore the World Wide Web and other sources of files and information on the Internet.

1 Internet FAQs

What is it? 2

Who's on-line? 3

What's in it for me? 4

How did it start? 5

How big?! 6

How do I find people? 8

Summary 10

What is it?

The Internet is not a single network, but a collection of thousands of computer networks, throughout the world. These vary greatly in size and in the number of computers that are connected to them. These linked networks are of two types:

- **LAN** (Local Area Network), covering an office or perhaps a campus;

- **WAN** (Wide Area Network), joining distant sites. A WAN may extend over the whole country, or even over many countries.

All LANs and most WANs are owned by individual organisations. Some WANs act as **Service Providers**. Members of the public and/or businesses can join these networks – usually in return for a modest charge.

The computers likewise vary from giant supercomputers down to desktop computers – PC's, Macintoshes, Amigas, Archimedes or whatever. They are owned and run by thousands of separate universities, government agencies, businesses and individuals.

There is no central authority or governing body, though there is an Internet Society, established a couple of years ago to co-ordinate and standardise rules of operation. The Internet relies on co-operation, driven by goodwill and enlightened self-interest. And it works!

Jargon

FAQ (Frequently Asked Questions) At every place on the Internet where you can ask for help, someone keeps a FAQ list. This is a set of common questions, and their answers. It is good form to check the FAQ first, before asking your own question.

Network A collection of computers, linked by cable or radio. On a LAN these can share the printers, modems and other resources that are attached to the network. On any network – including the Interent – users can communicate easily with each other, and share data held in each others' files.

Service Provider – an organisation offering access to some or all of the services available over the Internet.

Who's on-line?

Some would say "Everybody who's anybody", but that's not true – yet! So who is on-line on the Internet?

- **Academics**: Students and staff at universities, colleges – and some schools – throughout the world. These form the largest and most active group of users. Apart from the fact that they use the Internet for their studies, they will also not normally have to pay the phone bills.

- **Business users**: many multi-national companies have discovered that the Internet provides the most efficient and cheapest way of communicating with colleagues around the world. An increasing number of companies are also realising that it is a viable way to sell goods and services.

- **Government organisations**: some use the Internet for their own communications; some to make information available to the public. The White House is on line, though 10 Downing Street is not – at the time of writing.

- **Individuals**: anyone with a computer, modem and phone line can join the Internet through one of the public Service Providers. Millions have already linked up. In the UK at the present, around 10,000 new subscribers are coming on-line each month, and the rate of growth is increasing.

What's in it for me?

If you have access to the Internet, you have access to:

- **4 million host computers**, all of which are possible sources of information that could be useful to you in your work, your travelling, your academic research or your hobbies.

- **35+ million people**, any of whom could be future friends, customers, fellow enthusiasts, problem-solvers. There may well even be a few old friends out there already.

- **gigabytes of files** containing programs – including the software that you need for working on the Internet – books, news articles, pictures – still and video – sounds and much else.

- **a whole raft of services**, such as financial advice, stock market information, airline times and reservations, weather reports, small-ads and electronic shopping malls.

Where do I start?

Here, of course. Read on to get an idea of what's going on out there, then learn how to set up your hardware. After that, you should aim to get on-line with one or other of the service providers. There are examples of connecting to and using Compuserve, WinNET and Aladdin, in sections 5, 6 and 7, and a list of the current UK service providers on page 136.

Jargon

Host computer – one that allows Internet users access to (some of) its files.

Gigabyte – a thousand megabytes or 1,000,000,000 bytes. Taking each byte as a letter, this is the equivalent of around 2,000 thick paperback books.

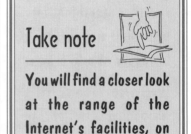

Take note

You will find a closer look at the range of the Internet's facilities, on pages 12 to 27.

How did it start?

Usenet – still a significant name on the Internet. The Usenet news groups make up the greater part of all the Internet's meeting places.

NSFnet – the (US) National Science Foundation's internetwork. The high-speed cables between its sites formed the backbone of the Internet in North America.

Appropriate Use rules – most of us are grateful for these, as they prevent us from being bombarded with advertising over the mailing lists.

The history of the Internet is interesting, but there is no room here to go into any details, and you want to use the Internet, not write essays on its history. However, there are a few things you should know, as they help to explain aspects of the present.

The Internet story starts with ARPAnet, a long-distance computer network devised by the US Government's Advanced Research Projects Agency. From an initial 4 computers in 1969, this grew over the next 10 years to connect 200 computers in military and research establishments throughout the US, with a few overseas links. It proved, beyond doubt, the practicality and the value of internetworking. By the mid 80's several academic internetworks,including **Usenet**, BITnet, CSnet and **NSFnet** had been set up. These combined with the research part of ARPAnet, to form the Internet.

The crucial point is that the core of the Internet was – and still is – government-funded research or academic organisations. It was not set up as a commercial proposition, and commercial activities on the Internet are a recent innovation. There are still **Appropriate Use** rules that restrict the use of the Internet for profit.

The second historical fact is that the Internet originally linked mainframe computers, most of which ran the Unix operating system. PCs, Macintoshes and other personal computers only came onto the Internet later. As a result, the Internet has a distinct Unix flavour about it. You can do everything from a PC – and there are some lovely Windows tools coming on stream – but sometimes you might have to use Unix commands.

How big?!

Because of the number of different organisations involved, no one knows for sure how big the Internet really is. Five years ago there were around 100,000 host computers connected to the Internet. It reached 500,000 by mid 1991 and has been doubling every year since. At the time of writing (late 1994) the total is something over 3.5 million – and these are just the *host* computers, the ones that provide services to the Internet.

If you look at the number of people who link into the Internet, either from their desktop machines or from a terminal in a large organisation, the best guess is that there are over 35 million of us, with more joining every day. If the number of users continues to grow at its current rate, everyone in the World will be on the Internet in about 10 years.

I don't quite think so...

Tip

If you feel overwhelmed by the sheer scale of things, remember that you don't need to know the UK road map to find your way from London to Leeds. If you keep your eyes open, you will see signposts to point the route, and if you do get lost, call out for help. There are lots of more experienced users willing to act as guides.

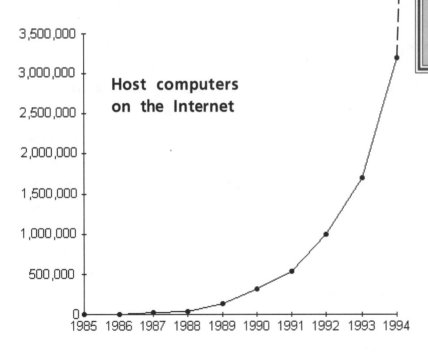

Host computers on the Internet

The Internet is growing so rapidly, this graph could be off the top of the page by the time you read it!

In the UK, around 100,000 people are already on-line from their home computers, plus many more through companies, universities and other organisations.

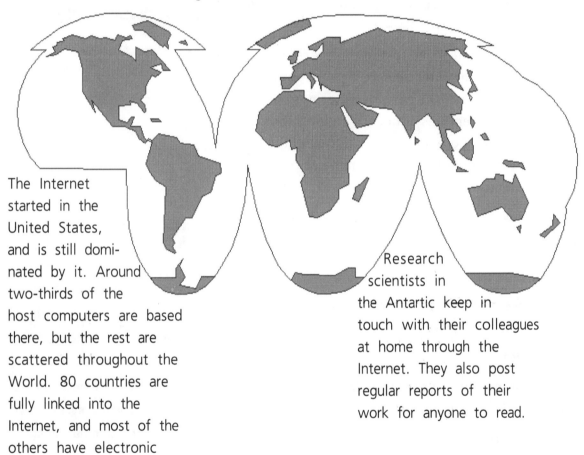

The Internet started in the United States, and is still dominated by it. Around two-thirds of the host computers are based there, but the rest are scattered throughout the World. 80 countries are fully linked into the Internet, and most of the others have electronic mail links to it.

Research scientists in the Antartic keep in touch with their colleagues at home through the Internet. They also post regular reports of their work for anyone to read.

How do I find people?

With something as large as the Internet, it is clear that you need a well-organized naming system to find your way round. Every host computer and network has its own unique name – it also has a number, but on the rare occasions that you need it, someone will tell you what it is. Computers and smaller networks within larger ones may also have their own names, and every user has an address.

Names have several parts to them, separated by dots. The parts are sometimes referred to as **domains**, and they are nested. The last part, or outermost domain, is the zone, which identifies either the country (outside the USA) or the type of organisation. The rest of the name is usually derived directly from the name of the organisation. For example:

vnet.ibm.com

The *vnet* network within *IBM*, a *com*mercial organization.

bhein.rel.co.uk

The *B*utterworth-*Hein*emann domain, within *R*eed *El*sevier, a *co*mmercial organisation based in the *UK*.

gn.apc.org

*G*reen*Net*, a member of the *A*ssociation for *P*rogressive *C*ommunications *org*anisation.

sussex.ac.uk

Sussex University (*ac*ademic)in the *UK*

oregon.uoregon.edu

The main *Oregon* site in the *U*niversity of *Oregon* (USA).

Zone name examples

com or **co**	commercial
edu or **ac**	educational
net	network provider
org	non-commercial organisation
gov	government department
uk	United Kingdom
aus	Australia
fr	France
ger	Germany

Take note

As the Internet links up many other networks which have their own addressing systems, some addresses are more complicated than the simple pattern shown here. If you come across an address that you need to use, copy it *very* carefully.

E-mail addresses

These follow the host name conventions, but with the user's name at the start, separated by an @ sign. Here, for example, are some of the names that I have had while researching this book. Notice the variations.

macbride@macdesign.win-uk.net

WinNet allocates domains (*macdesign*) to its users, as well as names (*macbride*).

mcbride@aladdin.co.uk

At *Aladdin*, users are simply given names.

100407.2521@compuserv.co.uk

CompuServe gives its users numbers, rather than names. As it has around 2.5 million members, numbering avoids the inevitable clashes that would occur with names.

These names are all from service providers, but the same conventions apply for people in commercial and other organizations.For example, if you wanted to e-mail my editor – perhaps to ask about some other Made Simple books – his address is:

Mike.Cash@bhein.rel.co.uk

URL's

Every file on the Internet has its own URL – Uniform Resource Locator – which tells you what it is called, where to find it and how to get it. We will be using two types in this book – for ftp file transfer (see page 16) and for the World Wide Web (see page 20).

Summary

❑ The Internet is a collection of **interlinked networks**, working together co-operatively.

❑ You may be able **get into the Internet** either through your business or academic network, but if not, anyone can get a connection through a public **service provider**.

❑ You can often find the answers to your problems in the **FAQ** (Frequently Asked Questions) lists maintained for most aspects of the Internet.

❑ The Internet gives you access to people, information, files and a vast range of services.

❑ **Estimates of the numbers** of networks, computers and people joined by the Internet can never be that accurate, as it is growing faster than anyone can count.

❑ Every network, computer and individual on the Internet has a unique **address**.

❑ Files are identified by **URLs** (Uniform Resource Locators). These show where the file is, what it is called, and what method to use to find them.

2 Internet services

Electronic mail 12

News 14

Netiquette 16

File transfer 18

Finding files 20

The World Wide Web 22

Gopher 24

Other services 26

Summary 28

Electronic mail

These are messages sent to other individuals on the Internet. Think of them more like memos than postal mail. A message can be easily copied to other users; and when you receive an incoming message, you can attach your reply to it, or forward it on to a third party.

The mail will sometimes get through almost instantaneously, but at worst it will be there within a few hours. The delay is because not all networks are constantly on-line. Instead, they will **log on** at regular intervals to deal with the mail and other services.

Key points about e-mail

● Every service provider offers **e-mail** access.

● The cheapest and normally most convenient way of handling mail is through an **off-line reader**.

● As with postal mail, to send someone e-mail you need their address.

(See *How do I find people?*, page 8)

Log on – connect to a multi-user computer, either directly or over a phone line.

E-mail – electronic mail.

Snail mail – the good old GPO.

Off-line reader – software that sends and collects mail from the service provider, and lets you read it and compose new messages after you have hung up the phone.

Take note

There are many organised MAIL LISTS on the Internet, each dealing with its own topic of interest. Subscribers can post messages to a central point, from which they are sent out in a block to all other subscribers. As a means of sharing ideas, they are very similar to Newsgroups – see the next page.

An example of mail seen in WinNET's off-line reader. This Windows software offers very comprehensive and easy to use mail-management facilities.

Messages can be stored in other directories

Call to collect and send mail

Options for dealing with incoming mail

This system also gives you access to newsgroups

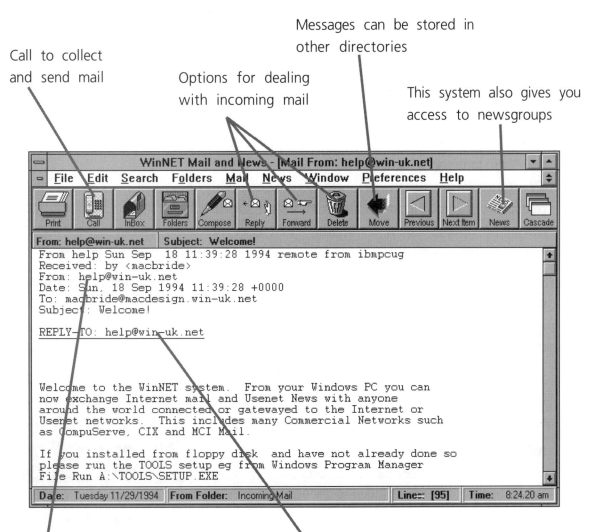

The header details the origins of the mail

Once someone has contacted you, it is easy to get back to them as you have their address. This one came from the automated help system. Most mail will have the name of the sender.

News

Thes have developed from e-mail, and consist of groups of users linked so that a **article** sent to the group is **posted** to all its members. There are thousands of groups, each dedicated to a different interest – professions and obsessions, programming languages and TV programs, software, hobbies, politics.

Key Points about Newsgroups

- Joining a group is easy, and free of charge and free of entry restrictions.

- The quality and volume of the communications vary enormously. At one end there are newsgroups circulating large quantities of interesting and highly relevant information; at the other there are groups where few people ever post, and even they are hardly worth reading.

- Some newsgroups are moderated, i.e. they have someone who checks all incoming articles before broadcasting them to the members. This reduces the quantity of irrelevant and/or boring post.

- Some groups are mainly for discussions, others are more like open help-lines, where people can ask for – and get – solutions to technical problems.

- As newsgroups bring together people who share a common interest, they can be a good place to make new friends.

- If you decide that a newsgroup is not for you, you can leave at any time.

Article – message sent to a newsgroup.

Post – submit an article for broadcasting.

Take note

Most newsgroups are part of USENET – the Users Network – a loose collection of individuals and organisations. Other old networks brought their own groups into the Internet as well. Not all newsgroups can be accessed from all entry points to the Internet.

Usenet

comp	Computing
news	Newsgroups
misc	miscellaneous
rec	Recreational
sci	Scientific
soc	Social and cultural
talk	Debate-oriented

Other

alt	all kinds of topics
biz	business
gnu	Unix systems
bionet	academic/scientific
uk	UK-based
... and more...	

Newsgroups are organised into a branching structure, with major sections sub-divided by topic. Their names reflect this structure.

For example, *comp.lang.c++* is in the *comp*uter section, which amongst other things covers programming *languages*, including *c++*.

● Join *news.announce.newusers* as soon as you get a chance. It is specially for those new to the Internet.

(See *Newsgroup subscription*, page 92, *Forums*, page 72.)

Drop-down list of main headings and keywords.

A good system makes it easy to find a newsgroup that interests you. This dialog box is one of the tools supplied by WinNET.

There is an **alt** newsgroup for everyone – including those who love the Flintstones...

... and those who don't

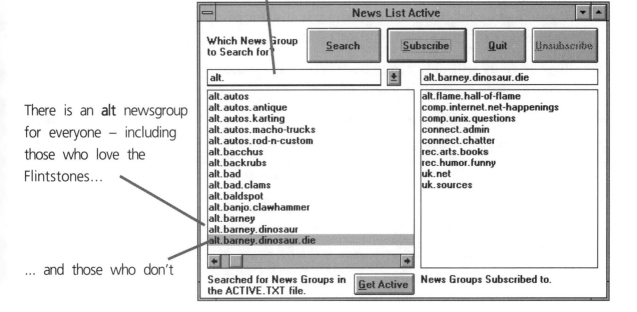

News List Active

Which News Group to Search for?

Search | Subscribe | Quit | Unsubscribe

alt.

alt.barney.dinosaur.die

alt.autos
alt.autos.antique
alt.autos.karting
alt.autos.macho-trucks
alt.autos.rod-n-custom
alt.bacchus
alt.backrubs
alt.bad
alt.bad.clams
alt.baldspot
alt.banjo.clawhammer
alt.barney
alt.barney.dinosaur
alt.barney.dinosaur.die

alt.flame.hall-of-flame
comp.internet.net-happenings
comp.unix.questions
connect.admin
connect.chatter
rec.arts.books
rec.humor.funny
uk.net
uk.sources

Searched for News Groups in the ACTIVE.TXT file.

Get Active

News Groups Subscribed to.

Netiquette

Newsgroups have their own etiquette, and you would do well to observe it if you don't want to be shot down in **flames**. The key is to remember that any article that you post to the newsgroup will be received by all of its members – hundreds, or even thousands of people – and that it will cost each of these phone time to receive it and personal time to read it. As some service providers charge for mail and article storage, it can also cost money.

If a newsgroup has 1,000 members (many have more), a 1kb article takes up 1Mb of net traffic and disk space. Even if members only scan the Subject line, and do not read it, the total time spent will be a couple of man hours.

Key points of netiquette

● When you first join a newsgroup, **lurk** for a while. Read its articles to get a feel of its flavour and level.

● Before you post any questions of your own, read the **FAQs**. These are usually circulated regularly.

● If you post a reply to an article, trim out any unnecessary text, to save everyone's time and **bandwidth**.

● If your reply will only really be interesting to the original author, e-mail it, don't post it.

● Keep your own postings brief and to the point.

Bandwidth – strictly the capacity of the comms lines, but taken to mean on-line time/ mailbox storage.

FAQ – Frequently Asked Questions, and their answers. A great source of information.

Flame – overreaction to a breach of netiquette or tactless remark. Can lead to **flame wars** if the victims believe they are right.

Lurk – read articles, without posting. There's nothing wrong with lurking.

Reply – send an email in reply to an article, rather than posting the reply to the group.

Tip

Join news.announce.newusers for advice for new users, and look out for Emily Postnews' Etiquette for USENET News Postings. It's circulated fairly often.

An example of an article and its posted reply,
from the *comp.unix.questions* newsgroup.

Your newsreader will
show the subject line
in a list of articles.
You can then ignore
those that do not
interest you.

The original article

Smiley! This is a joke.

```
From: magnus@thakhasis.solace.mh.se (Magnus Nasholm)
Newsgroups: comp.unix.questions
Subject: Re: protecting my e-mail
Date: 9 Dec 1994 19:08:14 +0100
Organization: Solace Computer Club, Sundsvall, Sweden
Lines: 12
Message-ID: <magnus.786995925@thakhasis>
References: <3c79fs$ji0@sparc.occ.uky.edu>
NNTP-Posting-Host: thakhasis.solace.mh.se

REPLY-TO: magnus@thakhasis.solace.mh.se

jackswe@ndlc.occ.uky.edu (Wayne Jackson) writes:

>I know of someone that can read my mail on the internet.
>Is there anyway to keep this from happening.

Don't send them to him... ;-)

No, but in fact it is very hard to keep users with the right
priviledge from reading them (root, for example). If it is a
unprivileged user doing this you should check the permissions
on your mailbox.
However I've got the feeling that anyone can listen to the
network and read mail in that way, at least in their domain.
```

Tip

**If you are joking, and want to make sure
that your readers know it is a joke, add
a smiley :-) or <grin> or <g>.**

File transfer

There are gigabytes of files are stored out there, just waiting to be **downloaded**. They include the latest updates of applications software, pictures from high art to low pornography, recipes, TV guides, news articles and all sorts of texts. Also there, are the tools you need for using the Internet, along with guides on how to use them.

Service providers have their own stores of files, and getting these is usually just a matter of selecting from a list. Once you are into the Internet, you have access to all the millions of other files on host computers all over the world. These can obtained by **ftp** – file **t**ransfer **p**rotocol.

Key points about ftp

● To do ftp directly, you must have an interactive connection to the Internet. This will let you connect to the host, search its directories and get files. (See *Go ftp*, page 76 and *ftp the easyway*, page 104.)

● If you do not have a direct connections, ftp can also be done by mail. (See *ftp by mail*, page 128.)

● To ftp a file, you must know where it is stored, and what it is called. (See next page.)

● When ftp'ing to a site, you usually login in as **anonymous**, giving your user name as the password.

Downloading – transferring a file from a distant computer onto your machine.

Uploading – sending files from your computer to the on-line host, for others to download .

ftp (File Transfer Protocol) – a nifty piece of software that can copy files between different types of computers. You need to be able to use ftp if you are to get files from anywhere other than the main data banks of your service provider.

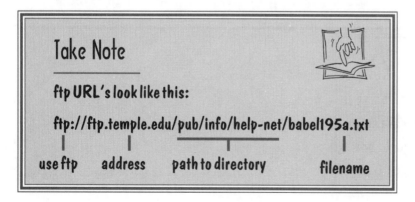

Take Note

ftp URL's look like this:

ftp://ftp.temple.edu/pub/info/help-net/babel195a.txt

use ftp	address	path to directory	filename

The URL shown on the left is for Babel, a glossary of computer acronyms and abbreviations. Get it, read it and baffle your friends.

This screenshot is from an interactive session using Aladdin's user-friendly ftp tool. It uses standard Windows techniques to change directories, and select files.

The remote system is at the University of North Carolina (unc), and I'm connected to one of their public sub-directories

This pane shows the directory and files on my system

Clicking here will copy the selected file into my system.

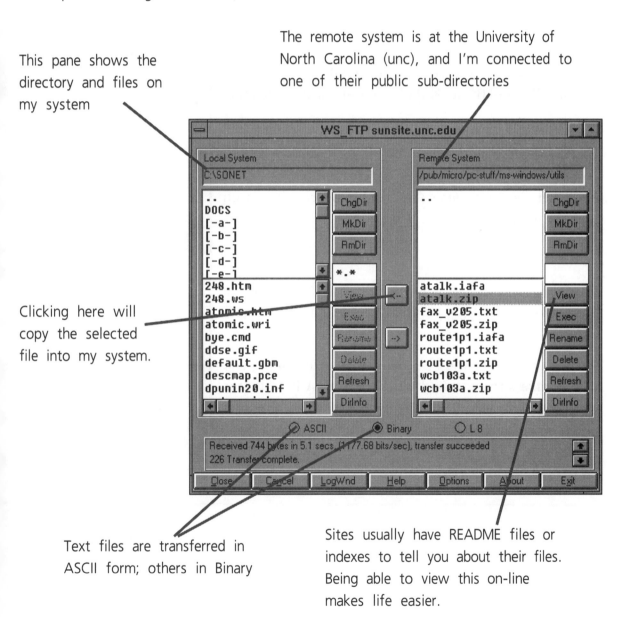

Text files are transferred in ASCII form; others in Binary

Sites usually have README files or indexes to tell you about their files. Being able to view this on-line makes life easier.

Finding files

This isn't as hard as it may at first appear. There are a number of ways to find files.

- **ftp** can also be used to tell you the contents of a directory, so once you have found a site, you can see what is there.

- **Members of newsgroups** will regularly alert other members of the arrival of a new and interesting file.

- **Browsing the World Wide Web**, you will often come across references to files, along with their ftp details.

- There is a program called **Archie** which will search the world's archives for you.

Archie

You cannot run this on your own PC, but if you have an interactive connection, you can **telnet** to an archie site and run it from there.

Archie can also be done by **e-mail**. You can mail a request to an archie server to find a file for you. A list of sites where it is stored will usually be mailed back the next day. (See *ftp by mail*, page 128)

Archie – a file-finding utility. If you know the name of a file, or at least part of its name, then Archie can tell you where you can find a copy to ftp.

Telnet – a method of accessing remote computers, to run Archie, play games or use other programs on the remote system. This can only be done if your service provider has an interactive connection to the Internet.

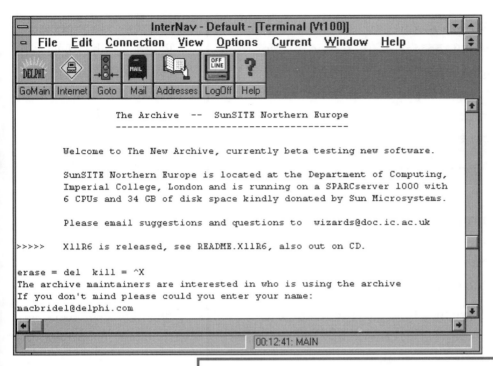

The start of an archie session over an interactive connection

Part of an archie reply to an e-mailed request to find uuencode, a program for converting binary files so that they can be sent by mail. Where there are several copies, you should get the one closest to you.

```
>> find uuencode.com
# Search type: sub.

Host nic.switch.ch   (130.59.10.40)
Last updated 04:13 25 Oct 1994

   Location: /mirror/msdos/starter
      FILE   -rw-rw-r--   997 bytes  11:07  5 Oct 1994  uuencode.com

Host micros.hensa.ac.uk   (148.88.8.84)
Last updated 03:30 29 Oct 1994

   Location: /mirrors/simtel/msdos/starter
      FILE   -r--r--r--   997 bytes  09:07  5 Oct 1994  uuencode.com

Host src.doc.ic.ac.uk   (146.169.43.1)
Last updated 08:30 31 Oct 1994

   Location: /computing/systems/ibmpc/simtel/starter
      FILE   -r--r--r--   964 bytes  09:07  5 Oct 1994  uuencode.com.Z

Host ftp.demon.co.uk   (158.152.1.44)
Last updated 03:14 29 Oct 1994

   Location: /simtel20/msdos/starter
      FILE   -r--rw-r--   997 bytes  08:07  5 Oct 1994  uuencode.com
```

The World Wide Web

The World Wide Web is a collection of pages, stored on computers throughout the world, and joined by **hypertext** links. It is the newest and the fastest-growing part of the Internet. Its rapid leap into popularity stems largely from the ease with which Web-browsing software, such as Mosiac and Netscape, can be used.

● The pages cover virtually every service and infromation source that is on the Internet.

● With a **Web browser** and some extra graphics/sound software, you can view pictures in exhibitions and live photographs from cameras attached to the Internet, watch clips from videos, or listen to music.

● Some pages have files linked to them, and these can be downloaded directly; others may tell you where to find interesting or useful files.

● To browse the Web, your service provider must be able to give you an interactive (**SLIP** or **TCP/IP**) connection.

Hypertext – documents linked so that clicking on a button, icon or keyword, takes you into the related document – wherever it may be. Web pages are written in **HTML** (HyperText Markup Language) – that handles links in a standardised way.

Web browser – program that lets you leap between hypertext links to read text, view graphics and videos, and hear sounds.

Mosaic – one of the first, and until recently, the best Web browser. Now challenged by **Netscape.**

SLIP – Serial Line Interface Protocol

TCP/IP – Transmission Control Protocol/ Internet Protocol

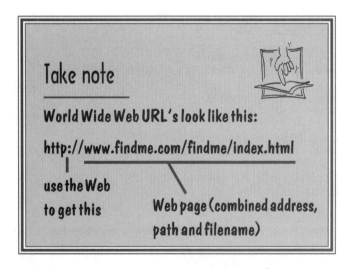

Take note

World Wide Web URL's look like this:

http://www.findme.com/findme/index.html

use the Web to get this

Web page (combined address, path and filename)

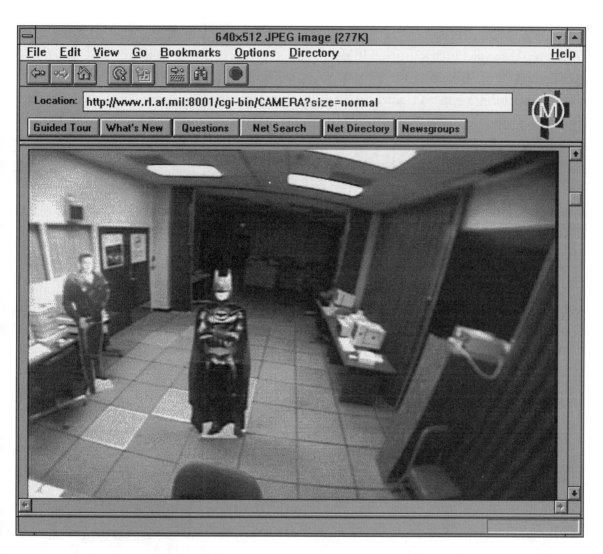

Location: http://www.rl.af.mil:8001/cgi-bin/CAMERA?size=normal

The sillier side of the Web. There are several interesting devices on the Web, including some 'spy cameras'. This picture comes from one at the Rome Lab. I haven't a clue what Batman is doing there.

Other devices include robot arms, a geiger counter, and a thermometer attached to a hot tub. The practical value is almost nil, but they are a marvellous indication of what can be done.

The software used here is **Netscape**, the latest Web browser (at the time of writing).

Gopher

Gopher is a **menu-driven** program that links many of the Internet's databanks into a unified information service. It was developed at the University of Minnesota, home of the Golden Gophers sports team and its name is relection of this and a pun on *go-for*. For a couple of years, until the development of the World Wide Web, it was the way to travel the Internet, and it still has some advantages over Web-browsing. The original gopher has been augmented by *gopher plus*, with some added facilities, and new Windows software for gophering handles most of the technicalities for you.

- The menus follow a standard pattern, with items leading either to the next level of menus or to items. You may sometimes go through many levels of menus to get to a specific article.

- Items may be text, graphic or sound files.

- There is a vast amount of information in **gopherspace**, but it's well organised, so that you can generally find what you want with little trouble.

- There are subject and regional catalogues as well as reference sources and *Gopher Jewels* – a collection of some of the most interesting gopher sources.

- If you don't fancy hunting through menus, there is a program called *Veronica*, which can track topics down for you.

- A good Windows gopher will handle the URL's for you – which is just as well, as they are not simple to manage for yourself!

gopherspace – sometimes used to describe the 1,000s of computers and their files that are linked through the gopher menus.

Menu-driven – where you select from a (numbered) list, often working down through several lists until you have focussed on the thing you want.

Take note

The huge quantity and high quality of easily available information in the gopher system, make it an invaluable research tool for student of all disciplines.

The screen from HGOPHER, a Windows gopher program. Selections are made by clicking on the name of an entry.

When you reach a gopher menu that you want to come back to regularly, you can record it as a Bookmark. Next time you want to go there, you can leap straight to it.

Back to the last menu

Article

Down to a lower level menu

Search routine

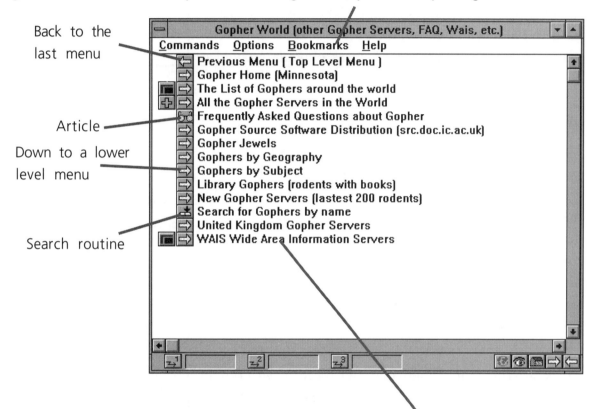

Gopher World (other Gopher Servers, FAQ, Wais, etc.)

Commands   Options   Bookmarks   Help

Previous Menu [Top Level Menu]
Gopher Home (Minnesota)
The List of Gophers around the world
All the Gopher Servers in the World
Frequently Asked Questions about Gopher
Gopher Source Software Distribution (src.doc.ic.ac.uk)
Gopher Jewels
Gophers by Geography
Gophers by Subject
Library Gophers (rodents with books)
New Gopher Servers (lastest 200 rodents)
Search for Gophers by name
United Kingdom Gopher Servers
WAIS Wide Area Information Servers

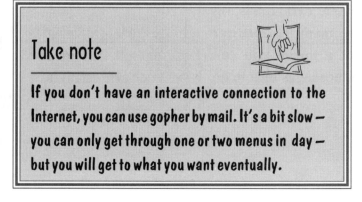

Take note

If you don't have an interactive connection to the Internet, you can use gopher by mail. It's a bit slow — you can only get through one or two menus in day — but you will get to what you want eventually.

WAIS – Wide Area Information Servers can be accessed easily through the gopher menus. WAIS does keyword searches through indexed documents.

Other services

Interactive services

Some of these are available to any user over the World Wide Web, others can only be accessed through a communications services like CompuServe. With a credit card to hand, you can book travel and theatre tickets, make hotel reservations, order flowers, chocolates, books, software and lots else besides.

Games

There are also interactive games which many people can play at once, pitting their wits against distant, unseen, opponents. The original, **MUD**, has now been joined by many others. At the time of writing, DOOM, a highly graphical, multi-level 3-D shoot-'em-up, is the main focus for most on-line games enthusiasts; with a multi-player aerial combat game also providing much excitement and frustration.

Chat lines

These are the on-line equivalent of CB radio, with typing replacing talking. The 'chat' varies from academic discussions to gossip between friends.

There is much overlapping between categories. In CompuServe, for example, there are many Forums for different interests. As a member of a forum you can download files from its library, read messages or join an on-line conference.

MUD – Multi-User Dungeons and Dragons. A role-playing game where on-line players cooperate or compete to win.

Tip

During the writing of this book, there was at least one recorded case of someone running a scam over the Internet, and you can be sure there will be more. Take great care over who you give your credit card details to.

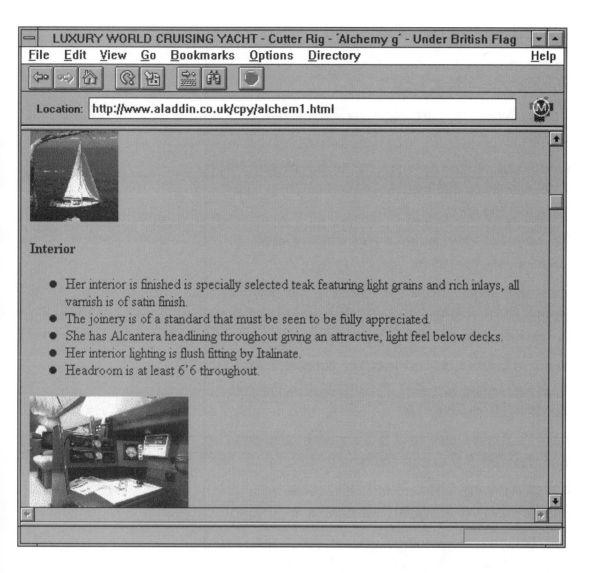

Yes, you can even shop for a yacht on-line. This is from Carl Phillips on-line Yacht Brokerage, a service run from Aladdin's Sonet. There are full-colour interior and exterior shots, with full descriptions of their stock. By the way, this little number is yours for a mere $795,000!

Summary

❑ **E-mail** is cheaper and faster than the post.

❑ E-mail can be sent to individuals, or to a group, organised into a **mail list**.

❑ **Off-line readers** are the most convenient way to deal with mail.

❑ **Newsgroups** provide meeting points for people who share a common profession, interest or obsession. There are thousands of them!

❑ The names of newsgroups are generally a good indication of their focus.

❑ Most newsgroups are part of **USENET**, and open to anyone. Some are run from other networks, and are not always accessible to all users.

❑ Lurk in a newsgroup and learn its **netiquette** (and its jargon) before you start to post, or you may get caught up in a flame war.

❑ You can transfer files to and from host computers using **ftp**, the file transfer protocol.

❑ The **World Wide Web** provides easy-to-use links between files on computers throughout the World.

❑ **Web browsers** are programs that let you travel read and view files on the World Wide Web. Mosaic and Netscape are the two most commonly used.

❑ **Gopher** is an earlier method of linking and locating files on the Internet. It is particularly useful for academic research.

❑ Games, chat lines and a range of interactive services are also available over the Internet.

3 Basic communications

Hardware 30

Serial ports 33

Parity and other bits 34

Data transfer protocols 36

Terminal emulation 38

Software 40

Modem commands 42

Summary 44

Hardware

To get on-line, you need three items of hardware – a computer, a modem and a phone connection.

The computer

Almost any type of machine is suitable. People are using everything from massive mainframes down to ancient Commodore 64s. For the individual user, life is probably simplest from a PC or Apple Macintosh, as there is the greatest choice of commercial and free software tools for these. Business users and students and staff in schools and colleges, will probably find themselves working with networked PCs or terminals of a large computer. These should not present any problems. Suitable communications software is available for all major networks and large computer systems.

If you only intend to use the Internet for e-mail and transferring files, a text-based terminal or a slow old computer will do the job – it will still work fast enough to keep up with the flow of data over th phone line. If you want to explore the World Wide Web, or play interactive graphics games, then you must have a reasonably fast machines that can of handle high-resoultion graphics.

The research for this book was done on a 486 PC, using Windows rather than DOS whenever possible. Windows make Internet working easier, just as it makes most jobs easier. Windows 95 – which may have arrived by the time you read this – should make things even simpler as it will have much of the basic connectivity tools built-in.

Phone connection

❑ All that is essential here is that you have a socket within reach of your desktop. If you haven't, any good DIY store will supply you with an extension kit and wall-mounted socket.

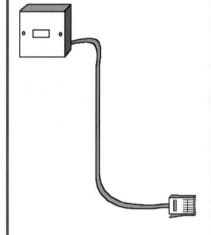

The modem

The type of modem dictates the speed with which you can transfer data to and from the Internet. The faster it is, the lower your phone bills will be, and its speed depends on two things – baud rate and data compression.

Baud rate

This is the number of *bits* per second (bps) that can be pushed down the line. The baud rates supported by a modem are defined by the CCITT standards (the V numbers). If you don't know what rates yours will handle, but do know its V number, look up the rates in this table.

Standard	Baud rates
V.21	300
V.22	1200
V.22bis	2400
V.23	1200/75
V.32	4800, 9600
V.32bis	4800, 7200, 9600, 12000, 14400
V.fast	as V32 bis plus 28,800

There are 8 bits to a byte, but all transmissions have extra addressing and error-checking information attached to them, so divide by 10 to get an idea of the *bytes* per second speed, or by 10,000 to get the Kilobyte rate.

300 Baud = 30 bytes per second = 1Kb every 33 seconds

9600 Baud = 1kb per second, approx.

Data compression

The same kind of data compression techniques that allow Stacker to cram twice as much data on your hard disk, allow modems to push data through faster. On modems, they are usually merged with error correction techniques. There are two standards – MNP and V.42bis, offering compression from 2:1 up to 4:1. Both are widely used, and many current modems support both standards.

Data compression does not always give faster through-put. It basically works by replacing repeated bytes (or patterns of bytes) by one copy of the byte plus a count of the repetitions. It therefore works best with text files, where blocks of spaces and repeated patterns are common. It does not work well with executable files, where repetition is rare, and if the file is already compressed then further 'compression' can actually make it bigger! Most picture formats have some sort of compression built into them, and many of the text files available for downloading over the Internet are ZIPped.

If you want to test the effects of compression, get a copy of PKZIP (see page 140), and try ZIPping files of different types. You should find that compression ranges from 90% or more, down to 5% - you may even find that some small files produce larger 'compressed' files!

MNP – Microcom Network Protocol.
Microcom is one of the leading data comms companies.

ZIP – extension given to files that have been compressed by the PKZIP utility. You need PKUNZIP, or WINZIP to restore these to their proper state.

Port – connection between the computer and the outside world.

Serial port – transmits data one bit after another down a single line. Communications are almost always done via a serial port.

Parallel port – transmits data one byte at a time, with bits travelling simultaneously down a set of wires. This is faster than serial transmission, but not suitable for phone lines. Printers are normally linked through a parallel port.

Take note

A 1Mb file will take over an hour to download with a 2400 baud modem, or around 7 minutes with a 14,400 modem using V.42 bis data compression. How much a minute do your phone calls cost?

Serial ports

All computers have one or more serial ports that can be used for getting data into and out of the machine. On a PC there are four, called COM1, COM2, COM3 and COM4. (COM is short for COMunications.)

A port may be a socket at the back of the main case, or reached through an expansion slot inside the case. If your modem is on a card, plugging it into any slot will give it access to the port. You may have to tell it which one.

- Most PC's have a serial port at the back of the machine. This is COM1, and the chances are it has a mouse plugged into it.

- Some PCs have two serial ports on their case. These are COM1 and COM2.

- A few have no external serial ports.

An external modem must, of course, be allocated the port number that it is plugged into; a card modem can use be allocated any internal port that is not already in use.

Take note

You will probably find that the modem's pre-set configuration will work with your machine. If it is, you will only have to worry about COM ports when setting up the software.

If you do have to change the COM port, you will also have to change the IRQ (Interrupt ReQuest) setting. See the modem's manual for details.

Buying a modem

- A 14,400 or faster model may cost more, but will be cheaper in the end.

- If it is Hayes-compatible it will work with almost all comms software.

- Be ready to pay a little extra for bundled comms software – but not too much as there is plenty of cheap / free stuff available.

- Card modems are easy to install, need no desk space and leave the serial port free.

- If you want an external modem, you must have an unused serial port.

- Note that you can only legally use BABT approved modems on public phone lines.

Parity and other bits

If you have ever played Chinese whispers, you will know that the message can get garbled when you cannot hear clearly. The problem is worse with data communications, for computers cannot guess meanings. Over time a number of different **protocols** have been developed to ensure that data gets through. One of the earliest methods, still in use today, was based on the use of a *parity* bit.

If you look at the **ASCII** table, you will see that the codes for all the normal text characters are less than 128. Now you can represent any of these numbers in binary using only 7 bits. As there are 8 bits to a byte, this leaves one over which can be used for checking purposes – enter the parity bit.

Even parity

With Even parity checking, the '1's in each byte are counted, before transmission, and if there are an odd number, the eighth bit is set to '1'. When the byte reaches the other end of the line, if there are not an even number of '1's, the system knows that an error has occurred, and a message is sent out. If the byte gets through intact, the eighth bit is reset to '0' to restore the original character.

Character	ASCII	Binary	Even?	Parity bit set
S	83	01100011	Y	01100011
I	73	01001001	N	11001001
M	77	01001101	Y	01001101
P	80	01100000	Y	01100000
L	76	01001100	N	11001100
E	69	01000101	N	11000101

- ❑ **Protocol** – set of rules controlling the way that communications are handled. There are many different protocols, so you must ensure that your system and the one at the other end of the line are using the same.

- ❑ **Ascii** - American Standard Codes for Information Interchange. The most common way of representing characters in a computer system.

Take note

Parity checking is not foolproof. If two bits are corrupted in the same byte, it will still be even, and the error will not be detected. Parity checking is only the first line of defence against error.

Odd parity

This is the same as even parity, except that the parity bit is adjusted so that every transmitted byte has an odd number of '1' bits. Either method will serve just as well, as long as the systems at both ends of the line use the same one.

Data bits

This refers to the bits in each byte that are used for holding data – typically 7 for ASCII text with parity checking, or 8 for **binary files**.

Stop bits

Some systems mark the end of each character by adding 1, 1.5 or 2 extra bits. (Yes, you can have half a bit as an electrical signal, though there is no way that you could handle it within a computer.) The extra bits do increase the length of signal for each character, but if they cut down errors – and retransmissions – then the overall volume of traffic on the line is reduced.

Common Patterns

Parity, data bits and stop bits can be combined in many different ways. The two you are most likely to meet are:

7-E-1 7 Data bits, Even Parity and 1 Stop bit.

8-N-1 8 Data bits, No Parity and 1 Stop bit.

❑ **Binary files** – programs, graphics, sounds, ZIP files and the like. If it isn't simple ASCII text, it's binary. If necessary binary files can be converted to a 7-bit form for transmission over 7 Data bit connections. One of the first Internet tools that you will need, is a decoder to convert these files back to their proper 8-bit form. Don't worry – there are decodes out there, and they are free, and easy to find.

Data transfer protocols

These protocols come into use when you are downloading binary and text files. They control the flow of data, checking for errors and retransmitting corrupted parts of the file. The basic technique is to chop the data flow into blocks, and perform a calculation on the bytes to get a **checksum**. The block and its checksum are then sent off together. The same calculations are performed on the bytes at the other end, and if the result does not agree with the checksum, the receiving system asks for retransmission of that block.

Common data transfer protocols

Kermit   one of the oldest and slowest protocols, but also a reliable one. If all else fails, try Kermit.

Xmodem   another old one, but reliable and in regular use. This works equally well with binary and text files. You will sometimes see it labelled **Xmodem/CRC**. CRC stands for Cyclical Redundancy Check, a mathematically complex, but very effective form of error-checking.

Ymodem   a development of Xmodem, offering slightly faster data transfer.

Zmodem   the main difference here is that Zmodem gives faster throughput and can cope with a total connection failure. With the others, if the line goes down during the transmission of a file, you have to start again from scratch next time you try to download it. With Zmodem, the transfer can pick up where it left off, adding the new data to the part-finished file from the previous session.

Checksums

❑ The simplest technique adds up the values of the bytes, subtracting 256 every time the total goes over that. This results in a single byte checksum. e.g.

Char	Code	Sum
S	83	83
i	105	188
m	109	297
		-256
		41
p	112	153
l	108	261
		-256
		5
e	101	106
Checksum		= 106

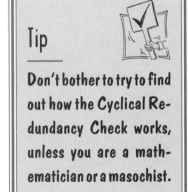

Tip

Don't bother to try to find out how the Cyclical Redundancy Check works, unless you are a mathematician or a masochist.

Handshaking

Handshaking is used to control the flow of data during the normal run of the session. It is needed because data may well be sent down the line faster than the receiving computer can cope with it.

There are three alternatives:

Hardware   where it is left to the hardware of the systems at both ends.

XON/XOFF   where the handshaking is managed by software. If the computer at the receiving end wants to halt the flow for a moment while it stores received data on disk, it will send an XOFF. An XON restarts the flow.

None   to be used where the other system does not use handshaking. You will rarely meet this.

Take note

You can leave the details of how these protocols work to the systems. All you have to do is make sure that the right ones are selected at the start of a session.

If your communications service does not specify which protocols to use, try XON/XOFF for handshaking and Zmodem for data transfer.

Terminal emulation

A normal terminal is a screen and keyboard combination connected to the main computer in a multi-user system. It has no processing power of its own, but sends data and instructions to the main computer for processing.

To connect to some on-line services, your PC must be able to behave as if it were a terminal.

There are three common types.

- TTY (TeleTYpe) – handles simple scrolling text only.

- VT-100 – can produce better designed screens, instead of just scrolling text, and can usually interpret some Function key controls .

- VT-52 – also has some screen-handling functions. Rare nowadays.

- ANSI – uses the ANSI codes to handle simple block graphics and colour as well as text.

Take note

When you send text down the line, the far computer will normally **echo** it back to your on screen. If it doesn't, you must turn the local echo on. It can be controlled by both the modem and the software. If lines of text appear twice, turn the echo off in the terminal emulator.

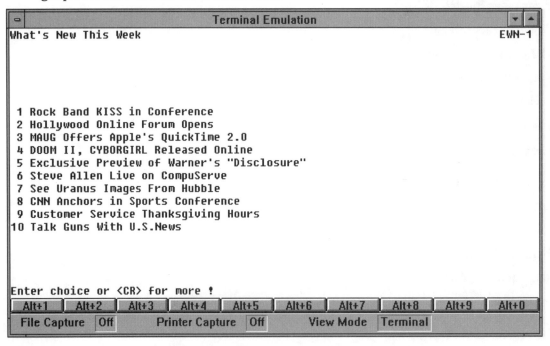

```
┌─┬──────────────────── Terminal Emulation ────────────────────┬─▼─▲─┐
│What's New This Week                                          EWN-1│
│                                                                   │
│                                                                   │
│                                                                   │
│ 1 Rock Band KISS in Conference                                    │
│ 2 Hollywood Online Forum Opens                                    │
│ 3 MAUG Offers Apple's QuickTime 2.0                               │
│ 4 DOOM II, CYBORGIRL Released Online                              │
│ 5 Exclusive Preview of Warner's "Disclosure"                      │
│ 6 Steve Allen Live on CompuServe                                  │
│ 7 See Uranus Images From Hubble                                   │
│ 8 CNN Anchors in Sports Conference                                │
│ 9 Customer Service Thanksgiving Hours                             │
│10 Talk Guns With U.S.News                                         │
│                                                                   │
│                                                                   │
│Enter choice or <CR> for more !                                    │
├──────┬──────┬──────┬──────┬──────┬──────┬──────┬──────┬──────┬────┤
│ Alt+1│ Alt+2│ Alt+3│ Alt+4│ Alt+5│ Alt+6│ Alt+7│ Alt+8│ Alt+9│Alt+0│
├──────┴──┬───┴──┬────┴──────┴───┬──┴──┬──┴──────┴──┬───┴───┬──┴─────┤
│File Capture│ Off │ Printer Capture│ Off │ View Mode │Terminal│      │
└────────────┴─────┴────────────────┴─────┴───────────┴────────┴──────┘
```

An example of VT-100 emulation, using ANSI codes to good effect. This is the welcome screen from the Almac service. With only 16 colours, and chunky block graphics, it is a little crude compared to high-resolution graphics screens, but it only takes 4k of data to create this sort of screen. Compare that to the half Megabyte or more of data that is required to create a high-resolution image, and think of the saving in downloading time.

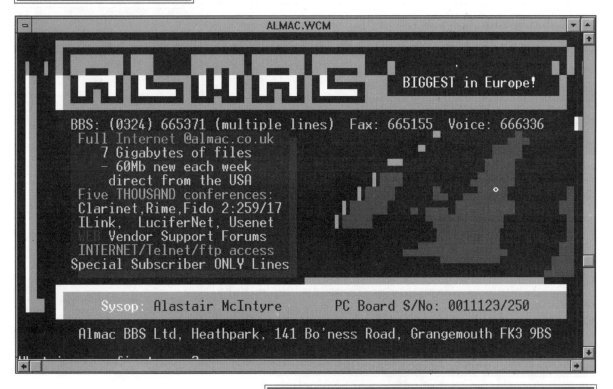

Almac can be contacted at Heathpark, 141 Bo'ness Road, Grangemouth, Scotland, FK3 9BS Tel: 0324 666336 Dial-up: 0324 665371, Comms Settings: 8-N-1

Software

There are three main types of software that are used for accessing the Internet.

- Basic Communications Software
- Web Browsers and other tools
- Providers Packages

Basic Communications Software

This performs the relatively simple (for software) jobs of controling the modem and the phone, and the interaction with the system at the other end of the line. This is enough to handle e-mail, file transfer and remote working with telnet and gopher.

Finding this basic software should not be a problem, nor should it be expensive. You may well already have suitable software on your system.

- If you have Windows 3, you have Terminal. This is simple to use, but effective. There are examples of it in action in Section 4, *Windows Terminal*.

- If you have Works or a similar integrated package, you should find a communications module in there.

- There may have been a comms package supplied with your modem. These bundled packages are of varying quality. In general, the older DOS-based ones may be technically very competent, but are rarely as easy to use as newer Windows software.

Tip

If you have Windows 95, you have all the basic kit to access the full range of Internet services.

The screenshot opposite is from Comit, a package bundled with Microlin modems from some suppliers. This is the opening screen, in which the settings of your comms services are stored.

40

Web browsers and other tools

To access the World Wide Web, you need software that can handle the links between the computers on the Web. There are several possiblities, and all are available over the Internet. You also need a service provider who can give you an interactive connection to the Internet.

There are many shareware and freeware packages available to handle ftp, gopher and other on-line work.

Provider Packages

Most service providers offer their own software packages free, or cheap, to their subscribers. As they make working with the service much easier, they are worth having.

These are modem commands. See the next two pages for more on them.

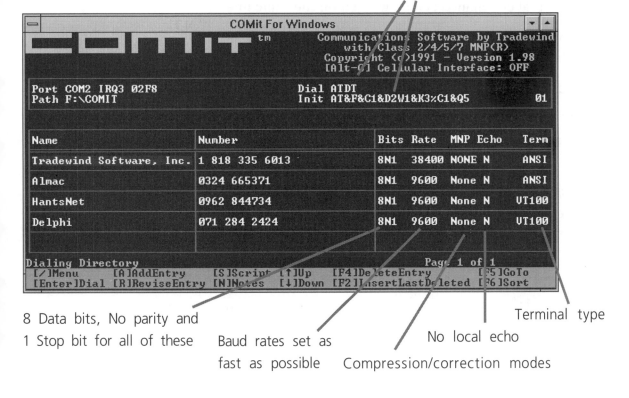

8 Data bits, No parity and 1 Stop bit for all of these

Baud rates set as fast as possible

Compression/correction modes

No local echo

Terminal type

Modem commands

With standard modem, a mainstream service provider, a decent comms package and a bit of luck, you won't have to bother much about these. So, the next couple of pages are for those of you who lack one or more of these, and for those who would like to understand a little more about what the system is doing for them.

Most modems will obey the AT command set. This was developed by the Hayes company and is found in all Hayes-compatible modems. It is a large and comprehensive set, but the few listed on the right will probably be all you ever need. They are used to dial the comms service, initialise the settings, and hang up at the end of the session.

● All start with AT – for ATtention!

● Several commands can be written on the same line.

● Some commands have a symbol (&% or /) before the letter.

Examples:

ATDT 071 284 2424

Dial this number using Tone dial.

AT Q0 V1 \N3 %C3

Typical setup string, enable verbose error messages, use error correction if possible and let the modem select the compression method.

AT commands

D Dial, followed by **T** or **P** and the phone number

T Tone dialling (used on all modern exchanges)

P Pulse dialling

H0 or **H** on Hook (Hang-up)

Q0 enable error messages (**Q1** to disable them)

V 1 verbose (full text) error messages

&D2 Hang up if DTR signal lost

\N0 no error-correction

\N3 try error-correction, but link anyway if distant modem can't handle it

%C0 no data compression

%C3 automatic selection of V.42bis or MNP data compression

+++ Escape (end session)

Jargon

Carrier Continuous signal to which a second, data signal can be attached. Data Carrier Detect checks that the underlying signal is still present

DCE Data Communications Equipment – the modem

DTE Data Terminal Equipment – a terminal or computer running terminal emulator software

DTR Data Terminal Ready, signal from computer to modem to say that it is ready to receive.

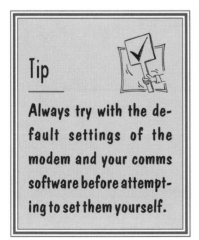

Tip

Always try with the default settings of the modem and your comms software before attempting to set them yourself.

Enable error messages

Error messages as words, not numbers

Turns on Data Carrier Detect when there is an incoming signal

Hang up if there is DTR drop – i.e. the computer-modem link fails

In this system, you can select a suitable string from a pre-written set.

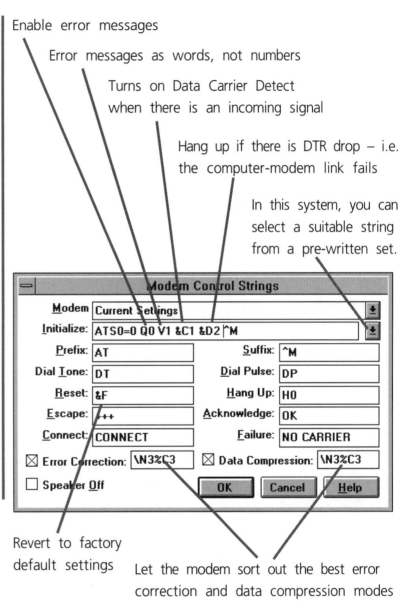

Revert to factory default settings

Let the modem sort out the best error correction and data compression modes

This screenshot is of the Modem command strings dialog box from Compuserve's WinCIM communications package. Most of these settings are still at their default; some have been changed using their user-friendly options; only for a few was it necessary to read the modem's manual!

Summary

❏ **To get on-line**, you need a computer, a modem and a telephone socket. Any type of computer can be used.

❏ **Modems** may be fitted internally or externally, and must be connected to a COM port. Most will simply plug in and go; some may need configuring to your machine.

❏ The **Baud rate** describes the speed of a modem. The faster your modem, the lower your phone bills!

❏ There are different **protocols** that govern the way computers communicate with each other.

❏ A key protocol covers the number of **data** and **stop bits**, and the type of **parity** used.

❏ **Parity checking** is a simple but effective way of reducing errors in data transmission.

❏ Files may be plain **ASCII** text or **binary** – graphics, sounds, programs and other non-text.

❏ **Data transfer protocols** control the way that files are sent between computers. Xmodem and Zmodem are the two most commonly used.

❏ You may have to specify the **Handshaking** method. XON/XOFF is the most common type.

❏ When linking to a remote computer, your machine may have to emulate a **terminal**. VT-100 is the normal mode.

❏ As well as basic **comms software**, you may need additional programs to access the World Wide Web and to make other on-line work simpler. Many service providers offer their own special software packages.

❏ Most modems are Hayes-compatible, and respond to **AT commands**. You may have to learn a few of these.

4 Windows Terminal

The Screen 46

Settings 48

Capturing text 52

Sending text files 54

Binary file transfers 56

Terminal files 58

The phone connection 59

Summary 60

The Screen

Terminal

A normal terminal is a screen and keyboard combination connected to the main computer in a multi-user system. It's *dumb* – it has no processing power of its own, but sends data and instructions to the main computer for processing. When you connect to an on-line computer, your PC must behave as if it were a dumb terminal.

The Terminal screen looks much the same as that of Write, or Notepad, but there is a crucial difference. Try writing on it and you will see. The normal editing keys and commands do not work.

In the Terminal, the screen is used to record your interaction with the on-line computer. What you type to send off down the line is echoed on the screen, and – of course – its communications with you are shown there. As the session progresses, the text scrolls up the screen and off the top, though not entirely lost. By default, Terminal will store up to 100 lines of text. This allows you to scroll back after (or during) a session to review your activity.

You can also capture incoming text through an option on the Transfers menu. Other options here and let you send existing files down the line, and send or receive binary files (graphics or programs).

Basic steps

1 Run **Terminal** by clicking on its icon in Program Manager.

2 Change the **Settings** to suit your computer and modem and the on-line service.

3 Use **Phone – Dial** to connect to the service, and **Phone – Hang** up at the end.

4 Adjust the Settings if necessary to get a working connection.

5 Use **FIle – Save As** to store the settings.

6 Next time you want to get on-line, just use **FIle – Open** and all will be ready.

Tip

Make use of the Receive and Send text options. Most people read and write slower than data is transferred, so working off-line as much as possible will cut your phone bills.

If you ever want to wipe the stored lines - perhaps to make room for a large chunk of incoming text that you want to retain — use the **Clear Buffer** option on this menu.

The Settings control how your computer talks to the on-line service.

Dial and Hang up from here

You can send and receive text and binary files with the Transfers options.

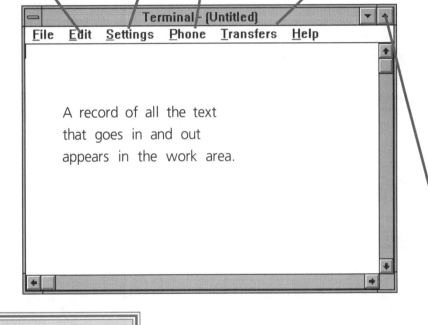

| Terminal - [Untitled] |
| File Edit Settings Phone Transfers Help |

A record of all the text that goes in and out appears in the work area.

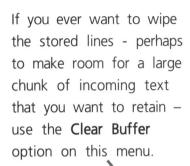

Terminal is best used with a full screen window, as most incoming text will be set to 80 characters wide.

Take note

Terminal may be free, but it's OK. Use it to get on-line. Once there you will find other — free but fancier — tools to download.

Settings

The **Settings** menu items define how your computer will talk to the one at the other end of the line. Following the rule "if it ain't broke don't fix it", only change those settings that you know you have to. Leave the rest at their defaults at first. They are probably OK, and can be adjusted later if necessary.

Four things must be changed or checked – the Phone Number, Terminal Emulation, Communications settings and Modem Commands.

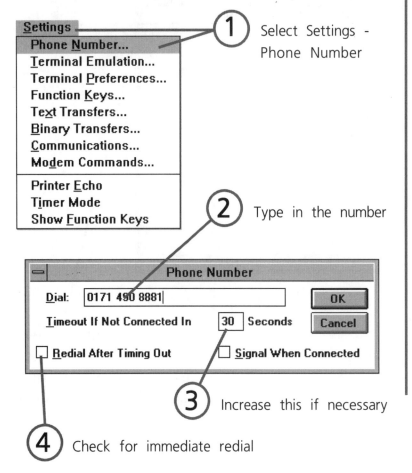

Select Settings - Phone Number

Type in the number

Increase this if necessary

Check for immediate redial

❑ **Phone Number**

1 Pull down the **Settings** menu and select **Phone Number**.

2 Type in the number. Spaces and hyphens can be used to make the number easier for you to read and check – the system will just ignore them.

3 The **Timeout** limit of 30 seconds will probably be OK, but if the service tends to be slow in establishing a connection, you may have to come back and increase this.

4 Check the **Redial after Timing Out** if you want an immediate automatic redial. It is often better to wait a few minutes and before trying again.

1 Pull down the **Settings** menu and select **Communications**.

2 Click on the fastest **Baud Rate** supported by your modem and the service.

3 Set the **Data Bits**, **Stop Bits** and **Parity** to suit your service. Typical settings are

7-1-E 7 Data, 1 Stop Bits and Even Parity;

8-1-N 8 Data, 1 Stop Bits and None Parity.

4 Select the **Connector**. This is usually **COM2**. (See page 33.)

5 Leave the rest and click **OK**.

Take note

The phone number and other settings given here are suitable for connecting to Compuserve's London node.

Before setting these, you will need to know:

● your modem's type, speed(s) and COM port number;

● the service's speed(s) and bit settings.

The faster the Baud rate, the lower your phone bills, but also the greater the chance of errors. Start by selecting the fastest possible and if this proves unreliable, change the rate for the next one down and try again.

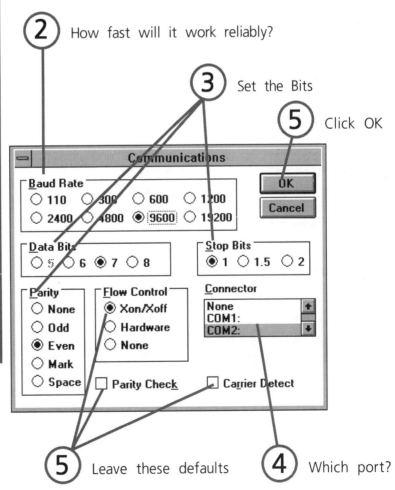

② How fast will it work reliably?

③ Set the Bits

⑤ Click OK

⑤ Leave these defaults

④ Which port?

Terminal

There are two aspects to this.

● You *must* select the type of **Terminal Emulation**.

● You *might* have to adjust the **Preferences** – but try the connection first with the defaults.

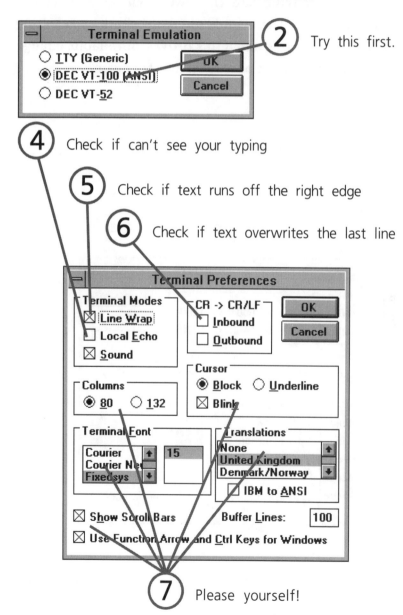

Try this first.

Check if can't see your typing

Check if text runs off the right edge

Check if text overwrites the last line

Please yourself!

1 From the **Settings** menu select **Terminal Emulation**.

2 Unless your service specifically tells you to use a different type, check that **VT-100** is selected.

3 From the **Settings** menu select **Terminal Preferences**.

4 If nothing appears when you type, turn on the **Local Echo**

5 If long lines of text are disappearing off the right of the window, turn on **Line Wrap**.

6 If incoming text overwrites the previous line, turn on **Inbound CR -> CR/LF** – this adds a Line Feed to the Carriage Return.

7 Adjust the remaining preferences to suit yourself.

Basic steps

1 From the **Settings** menu select **Modem Commands**.

2 In the **Defaults** box, if you have a **MultiTech** or **TrailBlazer** modem, select it. If not, use **Hayes** – its defaults will work with most systems.

3 For Pulse dialing, change the **Dial Prefix** to read **ATDP**.

4 Click **OK**.

Modem Commands

You should usually leave most of these alone – especially if it is all Greek to you! Increasing standardisation makes it possible for most of us to leave things at the default settings.

If your telephone connection is the old-fashioned Pulse Dial type rather than Tone dial, you will need to change the **Dial** instruction.

3 ATDT = Dial, Tone
ATDP = Dial, Pulse

ATH = Hangup

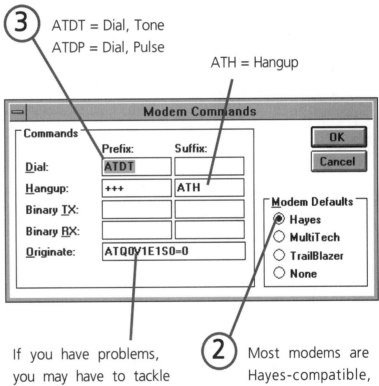

If you have problems, you may have to tackle this line. It controls the basic modem settings.

2 Most modems are Hayes-compatible, just as PCs are IBM-compatible.

Capturing text

Basic steps

Unless you have a very slow connection, text can come down the line faster than you can read it – and it can certainly go out faster than you can type! If you don't need to respond to incoming text immediately, the most efficient way to deal with it, is to save it as a file and read it later. If you have a long message to send, it is best to write it before you go on-line, saving it as a file, then send the file down the line.

● You arrange how text is to be transferred in and out, when you first set up a new connection.

● You can capture incoming text as a file, or send a file out at any point during a session.

❑ **Setting up**

1 Open the **Settings** menu and select **Text Transfers.**

2 Leave **Flow Control** as **Standard** unless your service provider tells you otherwise. The Standard option uses the Xon/Xoff method (see page 37.)

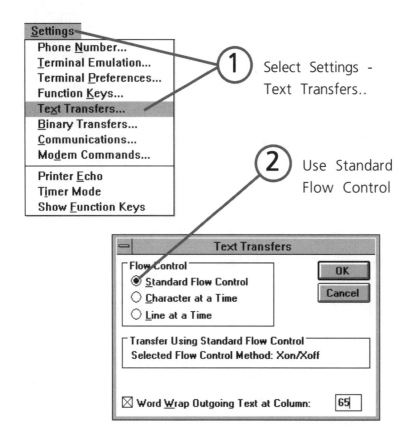

Select Settings - Text Transfers..

Use Standard Flow Control

Settings
Phone **N**umber...
Terminal Emulation...
Terminal **P**references...
Function **K**eys...
Te**x**t Transfers...
Binary Transfers...
Communications...
Mo**d**em Commands...

Printer **E**cho
T**i**mer Mode
Show **F**unction Keys

Text Transfers

Flow Control
◉ **S**tandard Flow Control
○ **C**haracter at a Time
○ **L**ine at a Time

OK
Cancel

Transfer Using Standard Flow Control
Selected Flow Control Method: Xon/Xoff

☒ Word **W**rap Outgoing Text at Column: 65

Tip

You can't do this until you get on-line, but find out how now, so that you don't waste time when it comes to doing it for real!

Basic steps

❑ **Capturing text**

1 Open the **Transfers** menu and select **Receive Text File..**

2 Change to the target directory

3 To start a *new* file, type in a **File Name**

4 To add text to an *existing* file, select it from the list and check the **Append File** box

5 Click **OK**

6 Start the text rolling in down the line.

7 When you have got all you want, click the **Stop** button, or select **Transfers - Stop**

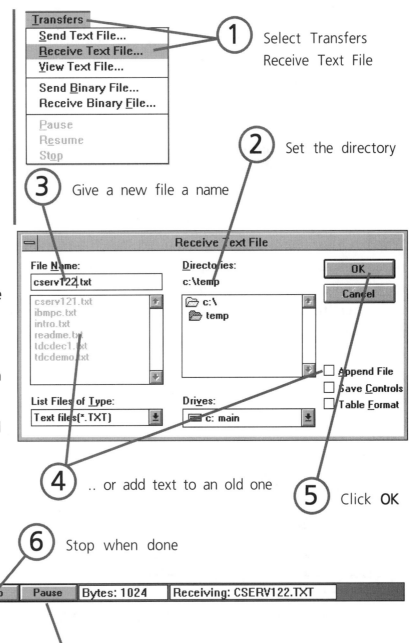

① Select Transfers Receive Text File

② Set the directory

③ Give a new file a name

④ .. or add text to an old one

⑤ Click **OK**

⑥ Stop when done

Pause suspends the recording, though the text continues to flow in. Restart with Resume.

Sending text files

Preparing messages off-line and sending them as files doesn't just save phone bills. It can also save bother. Correcting mistakes on-line, can be tricky. Because text is sent out and echoed back to you, there can be a delay between typing and characters appearing on screen – and between pressing [Backspace] and seeing them disappear. Just to make things worse, some systems do not recognise deletion. As a result, you have a fair chance of sending garbled text if you compose it on line.

Watch out for line breaks! A word processor treats each paragraph as continuous text, wrapping it round at line lengths determined by the width of your margins. When text is sent to a screen during a comms session, it is not normally wrapped and long lines disappear off the right edge. If you want your recipients to be able to read your messages conveniently, you must get Terminal to force line breaks.

Basic steps

❑ **Setting up**

1 Open the **Settings** menu and select **Text Transfers**.

2 Turn **Word Wrap** on, to force line breaks.

3 The column width should match that of your word-processor – typically between 65 and 75 characters.

(**2**) Turn Word Wrap on

```
┌─────────────────────────────────────────┐
│ ▬            Text Transfers              │
│ ┌─Flow Control──────────┐   ┌────────┐   │
│ │ ◉ Standard Flow Control│   │   OK   │   │
│ │ ○ Character at a Time  │   ├────────┤   │
│ │ ○ Line at a Time       │   │ Cancel │   │
│ └────────────────────────┘   └────────┘   │
│ ┌─Transfer Using Standard Flow Control─┐ │
│ │ Selected Flow Control Method: Xon/Xoff│ │
│ └───────────────────────────────────────┘ │
│                                           │
│ ☒ Word Wrap Outgoing Text at Column:  65│ │
└─────────────────────────────────────────┘
```

(**3**) Set a suitable column width

Tip

Remember to save your settings before you exit, so that you don't have to do it all again next time.

Basic steps

1 Prepare you message in your regular word-processor and save it as an ASCII text file with a .TXT ending. *Make a note of its name and directory.*

2 Start up **Terminal**, log on to your service provider and follow the normal steps for sending e-mail.

3 At the point where you would normally type the message, open the **Transfers** menu and select **Send Text File**.

4 Change to the file's **Directory**.

5 Set the **File Type** to TXT.

6 Pick your file from the list.

7 Click **OK**.

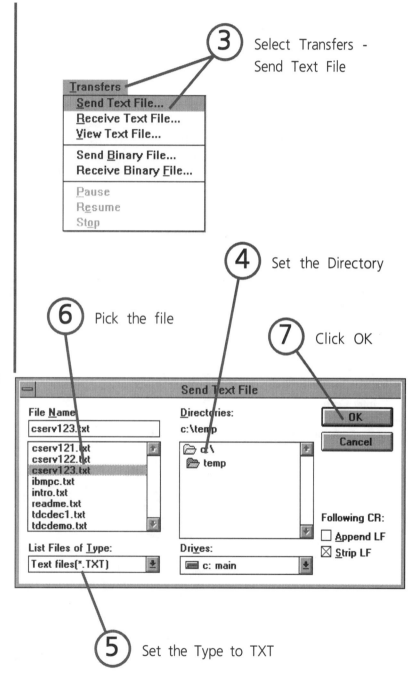

③ Select Transfers - Send Text File

④ Set the Directory

⑥ Pick the file

⑦ Click OK

⑤ Set the Type to TXT

Binary file transfers

Binary files are those that hold programs, graphics, sounds, and other non-text data. Downloading them involves different protocols, but follows the same pattern as receiving text files.

There are again two stages:

● Specify the transfer mode in the Settings.

● Set up a file at the point when you want to download.

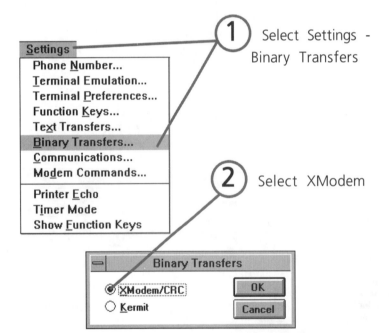

Select Settings - Binary Transfers

Select XModem

❑ **Specifying the mode**

1 Open the **Settings** menu and select **Binary Transfers**

2 Select **Xmodem/CRC**. Only try **Kermit** if Xmodem proves unsuitable in practice.

❑ **Downloading**

1 When you are on-line, find the file you want to download

2 Select **Transfers – Receive Binary file**

3 Set the **Directory**.

4 Type in the filename.

5 Click **OK**.

6 Back at the main screen, tell your host to start the download.

Take note

Many services offer their own specially designed communications packages, which will provide easier ways of doing many things – particularly downloading binaries.

Extensions

EXE – executable file, i.e. a program

GIF – Compuserve's Graphics format

HLP – Help file for a Windows application

JPG, JIF, RLE, TIF – other common graphics formats

ZIP – files compressed with PKZIP. You need PKUNZIP to open these out again.

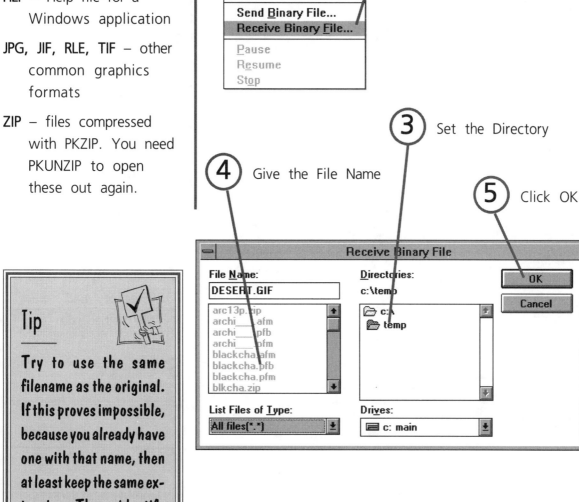

② Select Transfers - Receive Binary FIle

③ Set the Directory

④ Give the File Name

⑤ Click OK

Tip

Try to use the same filename as the original. If this proves impossible, because you already have one with that name, then at least keep the same extension. These identify the nature of the file, and are often essential.

Terminal files

Setting up a connection takes time, and you don't want to have to go through it twice, so, when you have worked through the Settings options, save them. You will find that Terminal adds a TRM extension to the file name.

Next time you want to conect to that service, open the file and you are ready for work.

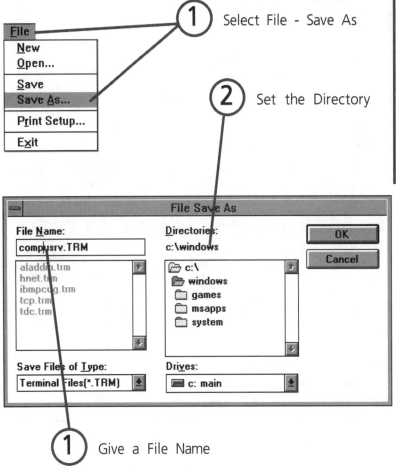

Select File - Save As

Set the Directory

Give a File Name

❑ **Saving**

1 Open the **File** menu and select **Save As**.

2 At the dialog box, make sure you are in a suitable **Directory**.

3 Type in a **File Name** that will remind you of the service you are using.

4 Click **OK**

❑ **Opening**

1 Pull down the **File** menu and select **Open**.

2 Switch to the right **Directory** and select the name from the list.

3 Click **OK**

Tip

Save before you try to use the connection for the first time – just in case it crashes your system.

The phone connection

Basic steps

❑ **Getting connected**

1 Pull down the **Phone** menu and select **Dial**

That's it!

At peak times, with a popular service, you may not be able to get through first time. Wait a couple of minutes and try again.

❑ **Closing down**

1 Log off from your service. You will probably need to type *BYE*, *EXIT* or *LOGOFF*.

2 Pull down the **Phone** menu and select **Hangup**

Making and breaking the telephone connection are the simplest parts of the whole business.

Two points to bear in mind:

● If there are other extensions on your line, check that no-one else is on the phone first. The modem makes an ear-bashing racket.

● Close down your connection to your service provider before hanging up the phone. If you fail to do this, you will remain logged on – and probably running up connection charges – with your service.

There are only two commands on the **Phone** menu – and neither has any options of any kind.

Take note

Most services will automatically log you off if there has been no activity from your end for five or ten minutes or so. Even if you do forget to log off, you shouldn't be running up huge usage charges.

Summary

❑ Windows Terminal is a basic, but adequate **terminal emulation** program.

❑ Before trying to conect to a service, you must configure the **Settings**.

❑ With a new connection, try first with the fastest possible **Baud rate**, retrying at a lower speed if necessary.

❑ Not all terminal connections works the same – you may have to adjust the **Preferences** to get the best results.

❑ Most phones use **Tone dialling**, though some still use the old **Pulse** method.

❑ You can **store incoming text** as a file, and send a file out over the line.

❑ You can **download binary files** via Terminal, using either the Xmodem or Kermit protocols.

❑ **Graphics files** come many different formats, of which GIF and JPG are the most common.

❑ **Save your Settings**, so that you don't have to do them again – and save before you try to connect, in case of disaster.

❑ When your settings are complete, and saved, use **Phone – Dial** to connect to the service.

5 Compuserve

Making the connection 62

Getting CIM 64

Setting up 66

Local nodes 68

Using WinCIM 70

Forums 72

File finder 74

Go ftp 76

Communications 78

Other services 81

Summary 82

Making the connection

At the time of writing, CompuServe is the world's largest on-line information service, with over 2.5 million members. It has been going for over 10 years, and over time has built up a very wide range of information and on-line services. With recent addition of ftp and the forthcoming launch of WinCIM 1.4, which supports TCP/IP and Telnet, CompuServe's members will have extensive interactive access to the Internet, and will make CompuServe the only global Internet access provider!

You can join CompuServe on a trial basis for a month and see how it fits with your needs. If you would like to do this, either phone for the introductory membership pack (details below), or dial up with your comms software and sign up as shown here. Have your credit card handy – its extended services are chargable.

1 Open **Terminal** and make the **Settings**:

Phone: 0171 490 8881

Terminal: VT100

Communications: 7 Data, Even Parity, 1 Stop bit

Baud Rate: as fast as possible up to 14400

2 Check no-one is using the phone and select **Phone - Dial**.

3 Wait for the *CONNECT* message, then press **[Enter]**.

CompuServe introductory membership kit offer

Call **Freephone 0800 289378** or +44 272 760680 (from outside the UK), between 9am and 9pm Monday to Friday or 10am to 5pm Saturday, quoting '*Made Simple Special offer, rep number 838*' and state your preference for Windows, Dos or Macintosh software. CompuServe will send you a **free** introductory kit, containing:

❑ **CompuServe Information Manager** communications software
❑ A **unique ID** and **password** to get you started straight away
❑ **$15 user credit** to explore **extended** and **premium** services
❑ **Free unlimited use** of CompuServe **basic** services for **1 month**
❑ **Free subscription** to CompuServe Magazine

* CompuServe is an international service and is priced in $US. Billing is in local currency at the prevailing rate. All queries relating to this offer should be directed to CompuServe at:

CompuServe, No 1 Redcliffe Street, PO Box 676, Bristol, BS99 1YN, England, UK

4 At the *prompts* type in these **responses**

Host Name: **CIS**

User ID: **177000,5606**

Password: **EXPLORE/WORLD**

Agreement Number:

MADESIMPLE

Serial Number: **93006**

You are on-line!

5 Follow the prompts through the registration process, taking the Basic membership option – you can change this later.

6 You will be offered a quick tour. Capture the text, so that you can read it at leisure.

❑ If you have problems, call CompuServe's Freephone support line on 0800-289458.

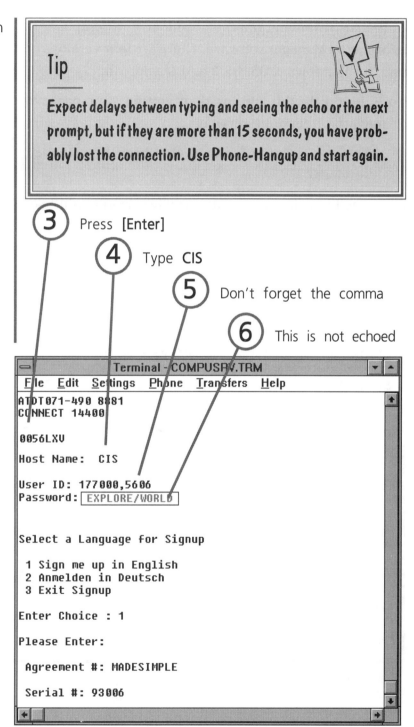

Tip

Expect delays between typing and seeing the echo or the next prompt, but if they are more than 15 seconds, you have probably lost the connection. Use Phone-Hangup and start again.

③ Press [Enter]

④ Type **CIS**

⑤ Don't forget the comma

⑥ This is not echoed

```
─                 Terminal - COMPUSRV.TRM              ▼ ▲
 File  Edit  Settings  Phone  Transfers  Help
ATDT071-490 8881                                          ↑
CONNECT 14400

0056LXV

Host Name:  CIS

User ID: 177000,5606
Password: [EXPLORE/WORLD]


Select a Language for Signup

 1 Sign me up in English
 2 Anmelden in Deutsch
 3 Exit Signup

Enter Choice : 1

Please Enter:

 Agreement #: MADESIMPLE

 Serial #: 93006                                          ↓
 ←                                                      →
```

Getting CIM

Once you are on-line, you can download the Compuserve Information Manager software. There are four versions of this, for Windows, DOS, OS/2 and Macintosh.

Note, if you do this, rather than getting your package through the freephone service:

● You won't get the $15 user credit for the extended services.

● The file is just over 2Mb. At 9600 Baud it will take about 30 minutes to download.

Enter choice !**GO CIMSOFT**

CompuServe Information Manager   *CIMSOFT*

1 CompuServe Information Manager for OS/2 - OS2-CIM(tm)
2 CompuServe Information Manager for Windows - WinCIM(r)
3 CompuServe Information Manager for the Macintosh - MacCIM(tm)
4 CompuServe Information Manager for DOS - DOSCIM(tm)

Enter choice !**2**

CompuServe Information Manager(Win)   *WINCIM*

1 Introduction to WinCIM
2 Hardware/Software Requirements
3 WinCIM Features
4 Order WinCIM
5 Download WinCIM
6 WinCIM Support Forum (WCIMSUPPORT)

Enter choice ! **5**

CompuServe Information Manager(Win)

---

1 No matter what else is onscreen, you should see the prompt

Enter choice:

If you are faced with

Press <CR> for more

keep pressing **[Enter]** (Carriage Return or <CR>) until you get to a *choice* prompt.

2 Type: **GO CIMSOFT**

3 At the next menu, type the number for the version you want – 2 for WinCIM.

4 Work through its menus and select the *Complete*, not the *Custom* installation.

5 You will be asked which transfer protocol to use. From Terminal, XMODEM is the best choice.

6 When you get the *initiate XMODEM receive* prompt, open the **Transfers** menu and select **Receive Binary File**

7 Set the **Directory**, type in the **Filename** and click **OK**.

8 Go and bake a cake while it downloads. Check the progress report in the status bar from time to time.

9 Press **[Enter]** when it is fully downloaded.

10 Type **exit** to close your connection and **Hang up** the phone

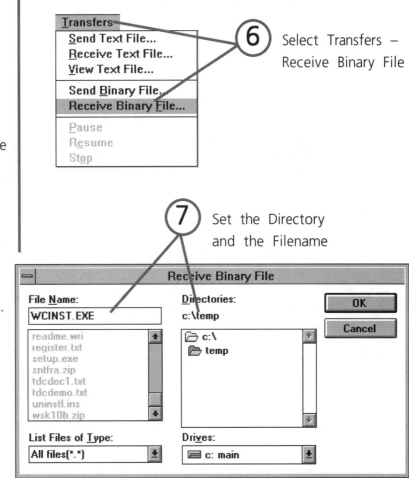

⑥ Select Transfers – Receive Binary File

⑦ Set the Directory and the Filename

⑧ Check progress

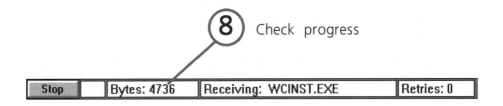

Setting up

Installation is straightforward – just run SETUP from within File Manager, and follow the prompts. This will create a CSERVE directory, along with a set of sub-directories, and copy everything into the right place for you. All you have to do then is put in your own details.

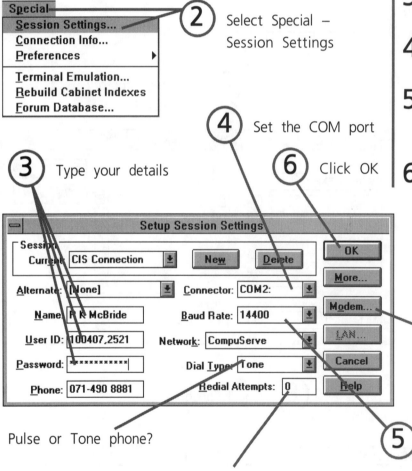

Select Special – Session Settings

③ Type your details

④ Set the COM port

⑥ Click OK

Pulse or Tone phone?

Set for automatic redial

Basic steps

1 Open WinCIM, but don't dial up yet.

2 From the **Special** menu, select **Session Settings...**

3 Type in your **Name**, **User ID** and **Password**

4 Set the **Connector** to the right **COM** port

5 Set the **Baud Rate** to the fastest you can, up to 14400.

6 Click **OK**

The default settings should be fine – leave them unless you have problems

⑤ As fast as possible

Basic steps

Preferences

1 Open the **Special** menu, and select **Preferences**

2 Select a set from the next sub-menu.

3 Set your preferences – largely by clicking check boxes on or off – and **OK** to confirm

Once you have started to work with WinCIM, you may like to adjust the Preferences settings to suit yourself. There is a set of seven, reached through the **Special – Preferences** menu. You can keep coming back to these until you have tweaked it to perfection.

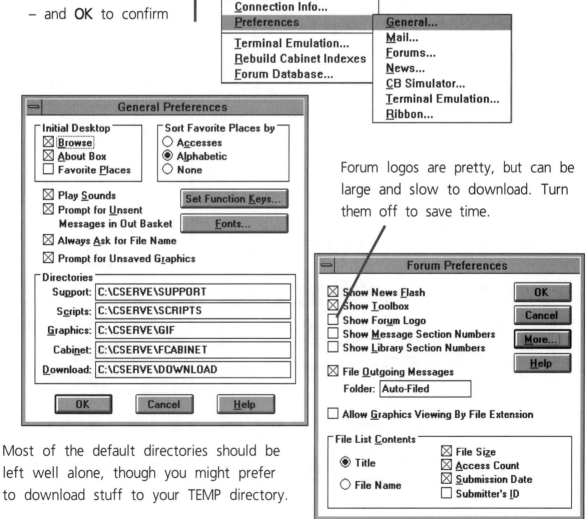

Forum logos are pretty, but can be large and slow to download. Turn them off to save time.

Most of the default directories should be left well alone, though you might prefer to download stuff to your TEMP directory.

Local nodes

If you live in the UK, your initial connection is to the main UK node in London, but for those who live outside the central metropolis, there is a network of local nodes in most countries. Check out your nearest node. If there is one in your local area (highly likely) and it can handle a high-speed connection, use it rather than the central node. Even if your local node works at a lower Baud rate, it may be worth using this if you spend more time reading or typing on-line than transmitting or receiving data.

Compuserve has a full list of its nodes in every country. They can be reached through the menu sequence: Member Support – Access Telephone Numbers – Access Numbers and Instructions – Access Numbers and Logon Information. The last level is called LGN-10. Knowing this, we can jump straight to it with the GO command.

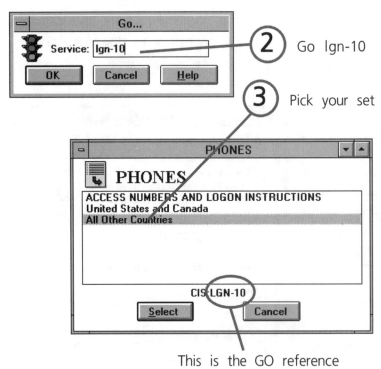

Go lgn-10

Pick your set

This is the GO reference

Basic steps

1 Click on

2 At the **GO** dialog box, type **lgn-10.** You will be logged on and taken directly to the **PHONES** panel.

3 Select **All other countries**. From here, you are working in the Terminal Emulator.

4 Give the first letter of your country, then select from the list.

5 Page through to find your nearest node, and note its number and baud rates.

6 Click ▭ to log off

7 Open **Special – Session Settings**

8 Click **New** and type in a name for your local node

9 Type in the **Phone Number** and set the **Baud Rate** if necessary

10 Click **OK**

(5) Note the details of your nearest node

```
 =                      Terminal Emulation                    ▼ ▲

          COUNTRY      STD
CITY        CODE       CODE   PHONE NUMBER  NTW  BAUD RATE
--------- --------   ------   ------------  ---  ------------------
Bradford       44     01274         841001  MER  300 1200 2400
Bradford       44     01274         840034  MER                9600
Brechin        44    013562           5782  GNS  300 1200 2400
Brighton       44     01273         550045  GNS  300 1200 2400
Brighton       44     01273         860028  MER  300 1200 2400 9600
Bristol        44      0117       930 4351  CPS      1200 2400 9600
Bristol        44      0117       921 1545  GNS  300 1200 2400
Bristol        44      0117       976 3265  MER  300 1200 2400
Bristol        44      0117       976 3243  MER                9600
Brodick        44     17030           2031  GNS  300 1200 2400
Cambridge      44     01223         460127  GNS  300 1200 2400
Cambridge      44     01223         250014  MER  300 1200 2400
Campbeltown    44     01586         552298  GNS  300 1200 2400
Canterbury     44     01227         762950  GNS  300 1200 2400
Canterbury     44     01227         762462  MER  300 1200 2400
Cardiff        44     01222         344184  GNS  300 1200 2400
Press <CR> for more !
 Alt+1    Alt+2    Alt+3    Alt+4    Alt+5    Alt+6    Alt+7    Alt+8
 File Capture   Off      Printer Capture   Off      View Mode  Terminal
```

Is it fast enough?

(8) Click New

(10) Click OK

Tip

You can reach everywhere through the menus, but if you know where you are going, GO gets you there quickly. Make a note of the references of any interesting menus.

```
 =                     Setup Session Settings

 ┌ Session
   Current: LOCAL CIS          ▼    New    Delete          OK

 Alternate: [None]             ▼    Connector: COM2:   ▼    More...

     Name: P K McBride              Baud Rate: 2400     ▼   Modem...

  User ID: 100407,2521             Network: CompuServe  ▼   LAN...

 Password: ***********             Dial Type: Tone      ▼   Cancel

    Phone:                         Redial Attempts: 0       Help
```

(9) Select the Baud rate and type in the new number

Using WinCIM

Compuserve appreciates that all its members are new sometime, and that many regard it as a tool to be used when needed and not the focus of their life. So, although it does have many sophisticated facilities for dedicated users, it aims to keep things simple. The WinCIM screen is a clear example of their user-friendly approach.

You will find many standard Windows items on the menu bar – **File**, **Edit**, **Window** and **Help** are much the same as in any other package. **Services** and **Mail** are dedicated to the on-line services. Most of the items on these two are duplicated by icons in the **Ribbon**.

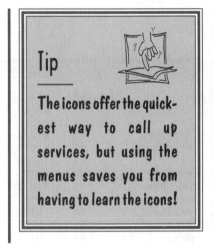

Tip

The icons offer the quickest way to call up services, but using the menus saves you from having to learn the icons!

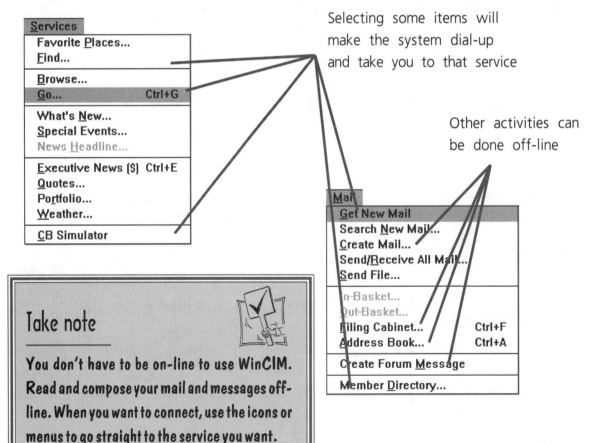

Selecting some items will make the system dial-up and take you to that service

Other activities can be done off-line

Take note

You don't have to be on-line to use WinCIM. Read and compose your mail and messages off-line. When you want to connect, use the icons or menus to go straight to the service you want.

Favourite places
– your own quick
access list

Browse –
through menus

Stock market
Quotes

Mail

Exit from
WinCIM

Find – key-
word search
for services

Go – to
a named
place

In-Basket

Weather
reports

Out-Basket

Filing Cabinet

Address
Book

Disconnect
from network

Help

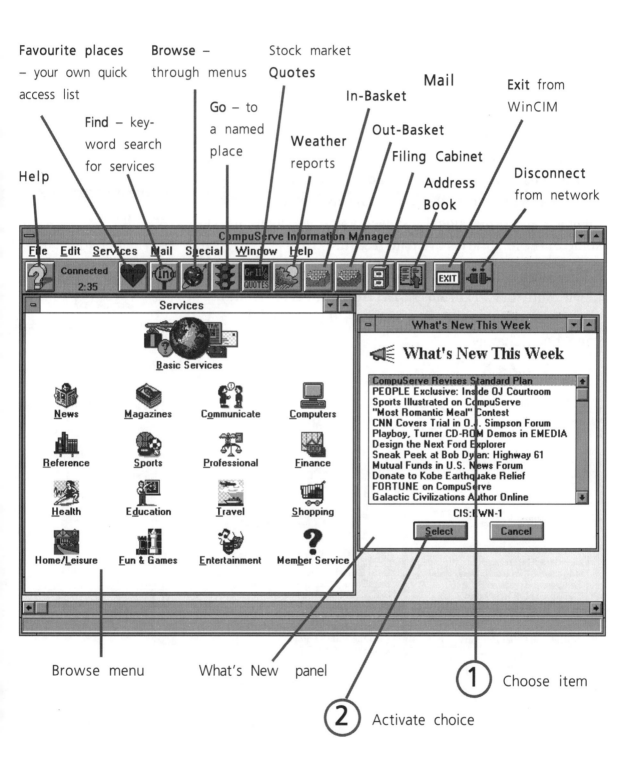

Browse menu

What's New panel

① Choose item

② Activate choice

Forums

Central to Compuserve is the use of forums – areas for members who share common interests. There are many forums, covering a wide range of interests, hobbies, sports and professional activities. Within each forum there is a Messages area, which serves a similar function to a Usenet newsgroup; a Conference area for on-line discussions; and a Library of files, contributed by its members. As the membership of forums includes many business and professionals, as well as skilled amateurs, some of these libraries are true treasure troves.

Before you can play an active part in any forum, you must join it. Note that all Forums (apart from the Practice one) are in the extended services, and your time there incurs connection charges.

Basic steps

1 Click on any of the Computers, Games, Lifestyle, Professional or Forums icons in the Browse menu.

2 Select a general area of interest from the top-level menu.

3 Highlight a forum in the list.

4 Click [Select]

Takenote

+ after a name shows that the forum is in extended services. GO RATES to see the charges.

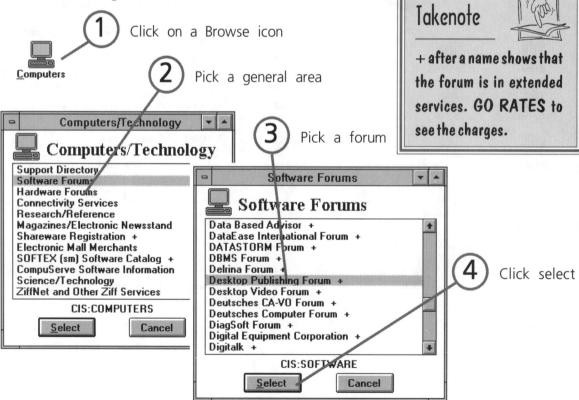

Click on a Browse icon

Computers

Pick a general area

Computers/Technology

Support Directory
Software Forums
Hardware Forums
Connectivity Services
Research/Reference
Magazines/Electronic Newsstand
Shareware Registration +
Electronic Mall Merchants
SOFTEX (sm) Software Catalog +
CompuServe Software Information
Science/Technology
ZiffNet and Other Ziff Services

CIS:COMPUTERS

[Select]   [Cancel]

Pick a forum

Software Forums

Data Based Advisor +
DataEase International Forum +
DATASTORM Forum +
DBMS Forum +
Delrina Forum +
Desktop Publishing Forum +
Desktop Video Forum +
Deutsches CA-VO Forum +
Deutsches Computer Forum +
DiagSoft Forum +
Digital Equipment Corporation +
Digitalk +

CIS:SOFTWARE

[Select]   [Cancel]

Click select

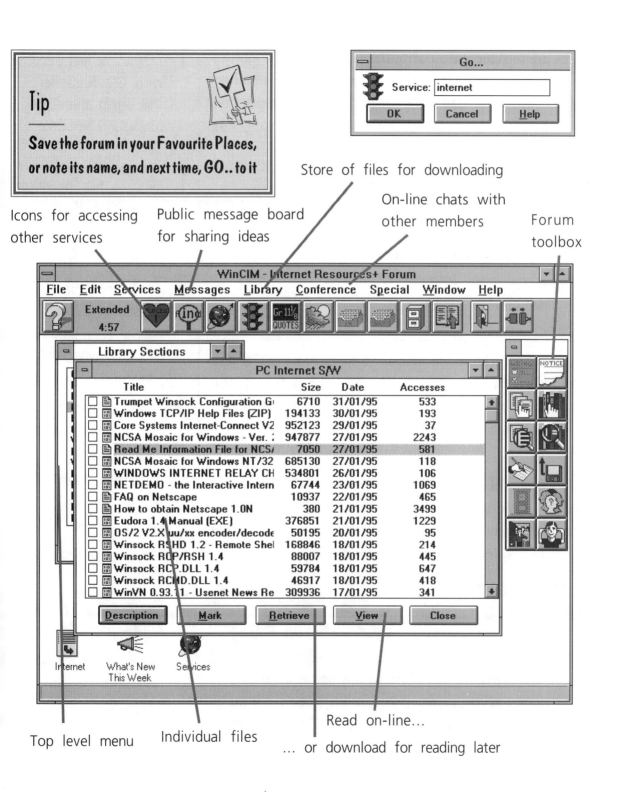

Tip

Save the forum in your Favourite Places, or note its name, and next time, GO.. to it

Go...

Service: internet

OK   Cancel   Help

Store of files for downloading

On-line chats with other members

Forum toolbox

Icons for accessing other services

Public message board for sharing ideas

WinCIM - Internet Resources+ Forum

File Edit Services Messages Library Conference Special Window Help

Extended
4:57

Library Sections

PC Internet S/W

Title	Size	Date	Accesses
Trumpet Winsock Configuration G	6710	31/01/95	533
Windows TCP/IP Help Files (ZIP)	194133	30/01/95	193
Core Systems Internet-Connect V2	952123	29/01/95	37
NCSA Mosaic for Windows - Ver. 2	947877	27/01/95	2243
Read Me Information File for NCS/	7050	27/01/95	581
NCSA Mosaic for Windows NT/32	685130	27/01/95	118
WINDOWS INTERNET RELAY CH	534801	26/01/95	106
NETDEMO - the Interactive Intern	67744	23/01/95	1069
FAQ on Netscape	10937	22/01/95	465
How to obtain Netscape 1.0N	380	21/01/95	3499
Eudora 1.4 Manual (EXE)	376851	21/01/95	1229
OS/2 V2.X uu/xx encoder/decode	50195	20/01/95	95
Winsock RSHD 1.2 - Remote Shel	168846	18/01/95	214
Winsock RCP/RSH 1.4	88007	18/01/95	445
Winsock RCP.DLL 1.4	59784	18/01/95	647
Winsock RCMD.DLL 1.4	46917	18/01/95	418
WinVN 0.93.11 - Usenet News Re	309936	17/01/95	341

Description   Mark   Retrieve   View   Close

Internet   What's New   Services
           This Week

Read on-line...

Top level menu   Individual files   ... or download for reading later

73

File finder

If you are looking for a particular file, and don't want to have to hunt through forum libraries for it, try File Finder. You don't even have to know the file's name – though that helps. You can search Compuserve's databases using any one or a combination of:

- Keyword
- Submission date
- Forum
- File Type e.g. ASCII, binary
- Extension e.g. EXE, ZIP, COM, TXT
- File name
- Submitter

Wildcards can be used, just as they can in MSDOS and Windows, with * standing for unknown characters. In the example, we are looking for PKZIP, the file compression program, using this :

    PKZIP*.*

This will find anything that starts with PKZIP, whatever else the name includes, and whatever the extension. In fact, it turns up three copies of PKZIP.EXE and one of PXZIP.TXT, a text on compression utilities.

Tip

Two other files are well worth finding and downloading: PKUNZIP.EXE, the uncompressor, and WNMAIL24.ZIP, the program to use with WinNet – see the next section.

Basic steps

1 Jump to the first menu with **GO filefinder** and select the Finder for your computer

or for PC users

1 Jump to PC File finder with **GO pcff**

2 Select **Access File Finder**

3 At the next panel, choose your search criteria, e.g. **File Name** and give what detail you can

4 Start the search.

5 The **Access** panel will then have a note of many files have been found, and a **Display** option - select it.

6 Select a file from the Display list

7 [Retrieve] it, (see page 60 for downloading)

8 Close the panels to return to the top menu, or pull the plug with

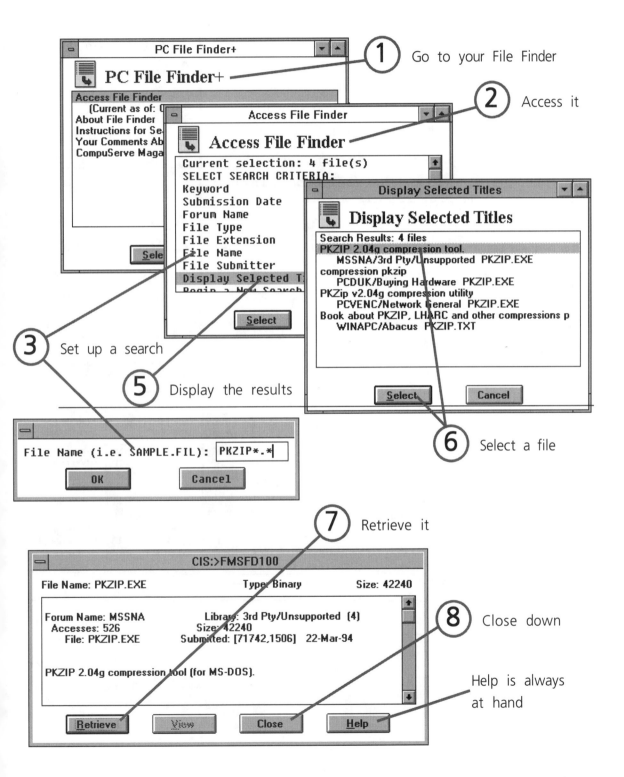

PC File Finder+

(1) Go to your File Finder

Access File Finder
(Current as of: (
About File Finder
Instructions for Se
Your Comments Ab
CompuServe Maga

Access File Finder

(2) Access it

Current selection: 4 file(s)
SELECT SEARCH CRITERIA:
Keyword
Submission Date
Forum Name
File Type
File Extension
File Name
File Submitter
Display Selected T
Begin a New Search

Select

Display Selected Titles

Search Results: 4 files
PKZIP 2.04g compression tool.
    MSSNA/3rd Pty/Unsupported PKZIP.EXE
compression pkzip
    PCDUK/Buying Hardware PKZIP.EXE
PKZip v2.04g compression utility
    PCVENC/Network General PKZIP.EXE
Book about PKZIP, LHARC and other compressions p
    WINAPC/Abacus PKZIP.TXT

Select   Cancel

(3) Set up a search

(5) Display the results

(6) Select a file

File Name (i.e. SAMPLE.FIL): PKZIP*.*

OK   Cancel

(7) Retrieve it

CIS:>FMSFD100

File Name: PKZIP.EXE   Type: Binary   Size: 42240

Forum Name: MSSNA   Library: 3rd Pty/Unsupported (4)
  Accesses: 526   Size: 42240
    File: PKZIP.EXE   Submitted: [71742,1506] 22-Mar-94

PKZIP 2.04g compression tool (for MS-DOS).

Retrieve   View   Close   Help

(8) Close down

Help is always
at hand

Go ftp

ftp – file transfer protocol – is the tool that allows you to get files from host machines anywhere on the Internet. Compuserve's implementation makes it simple. If you have got the URL, you can get the file. Even if you have not got a URL, you can browse and see what's available.

The system is set up for the normal *anonymous* login, with your internet address (*User ID@compuserve.com*) as the password. This will be correct for almost all sites.

❑ **Getting there**

1 Go ftp

either browse

2 Select Popular Sites

3 Pick a site from the list

or if you know the URL

2 Access a Specific Site

3 Type the site name and the directory

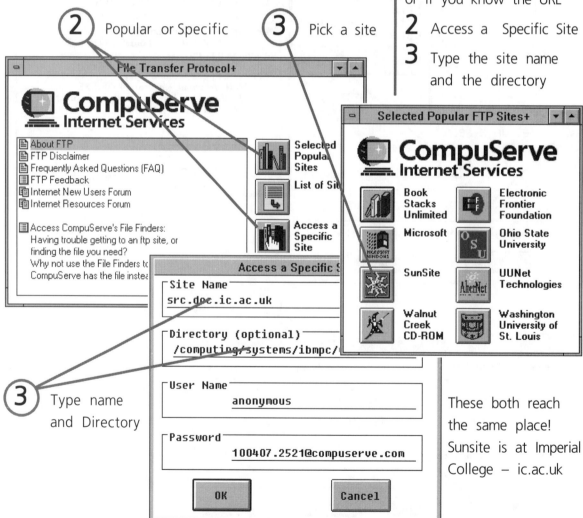

② Popular or Specific

③ Pick a site

③ Type name and Directory

These both reach the same place! Sunsite is at Imperial College – ic.ac.uk

76

Basic steps

❑ **Working on-site**

1 Change directories if necessary

2 Select and **View** any README file – they are always worth it

3 Select and **Retrieve** the file you want.

4 Repeat for any other files then **Leave**

Take note

Copies of many of the most popular files are stored on Compuserve's computers. Take the strain off the Internet connections and download from Compuserve if you can. To check their files, GO filefinder.

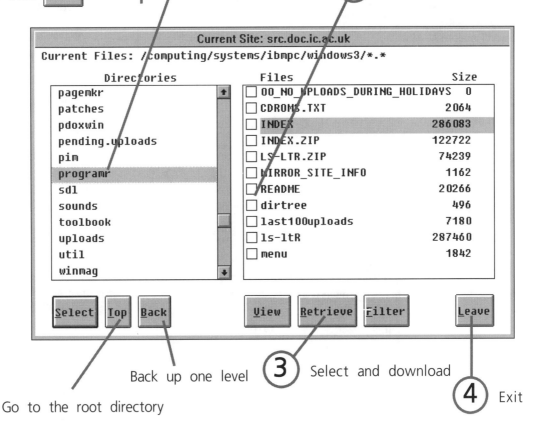

① Set the Directory

② View README

Current Site: src.doc.ic.ac.uk

Current Files: /computing/systems/ibmpc/windows3/*.*

Directories	Files	Size
pagemkr	☐ 00_NO_UPLOADS_DURING_HOLIDAYS	0
patches	☐ CDROMS.TXT	2064
pdoxwin	☐ INDEX	286083
pending.uploads	☐ INDEX.ZIP	122722
pim	☐ LS-LTR.ZIP	74239
programr	☐ MIRROR_SITE_INFO	1162
sdl	☐ README	20266
sounds	☐ dirtree	496
toolbook	☐ last100uploads	7180
uploads	☐ ls-ltR	287460
util	☐ menu	1842
winmag		

Select **Top** **Back**   **View** **Retrieve** **Filter**   **Leave**

Back up one level   ③ Select and download

Go to the root directory

④ Exit

77

Communications

Communicate

Creating Mail

Mail can be composed and read either off- or on-line. You will probably find, that it is simplest to scan incoming mail, and reply to brief notes while on-line, but to deal with longer ones after you have logged off.

WinCIM has its own editor for creating mail, but you can, if you prefer, write your messages in your favourite word-processor, save them as text files, and then send the files through the mail system.

1 Select **Create Mail...** from the **Mail** menu

2 If the recipient is in your **Address Book**, select the name and [Copy >>] it into the **Recipient** list,

otherwise

Type in the name and e-mail address, and click [<< Copy] to add to your Address Book

3 If you want to send copies to others, add their names when **CC** is highlighted

4 Click **OK**

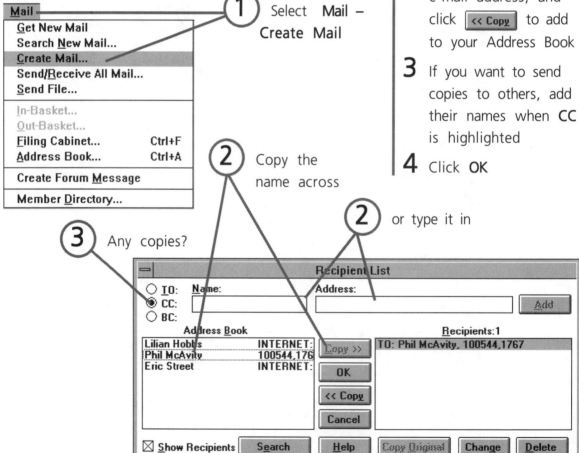

Select **Mail – Create Mail**

Copy the name across

or type it in

Any copies?

78

5 Type a **Subject** line – this alerts the recipient to the content of the mail (see next page)

6 Type your message, using the usual WIndows techniques to edit it.

7 Click [Send Now] – the system will log you on, if you are off-line, and send it.

Names are for human use, so write these to suit yourself; **Addresses** are for the e-mail system, and must be exact.

● If the recipient is another Compuserve member, all you need is the User ID. For Phil McAvity, in the example, the address is 100544,1767

● If the recipient is elsewhere on the Internet, the address must start with *INTERNET:* and have the full *name@domain* address, e.g.

   INTERNET:macbride@macdesign.win-uk.net

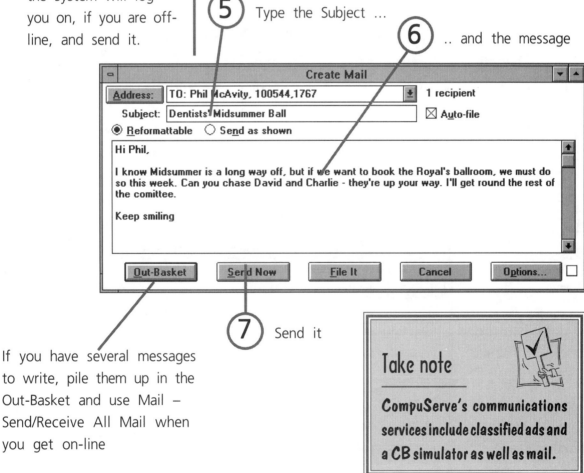

⑤ Type the Subject ...

⑥ .. and the message

⑦ Send it

If you have several messages to write, pile them up in the Out-Basket and use Mail – Send/Receive All Mail when you get on-line

Take note

CompuServe's communications services include classified ads and a CB simulator as well as mail.

Getting mail

Incoming messages are stored in your mailbox at CompuServe. If there are any, you will see a **mail messages waiting** prompt when you log in. Get them. If you set the **Preferences – Mail** to *Delete Retrieved Messages*, getting them will delete them from your mailbox. After reading your messages, either delete them or file them on your own machine. Other options in the reading window allow you to reply, or to forward the mail to a third party – perhaps after adding some comments.

1 Open the **Mail** menu and select **Get New Mail**.

2 Scan the subject lines to see what the messages are about.

3 [Get] individual messages or [Get All] your mail at once.

4 Read you new mail and deal with it.

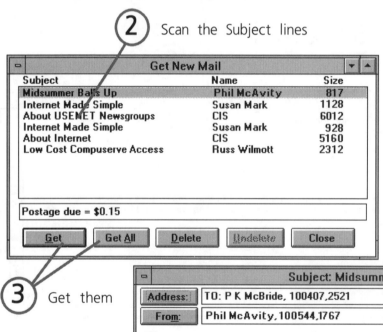

② Scan the Subject lines

③ Get them

Tip

Check your mailbox regularly. If you let it clog up with old mail you will start to incur storage charges.

④ Respond

Click to get the next message

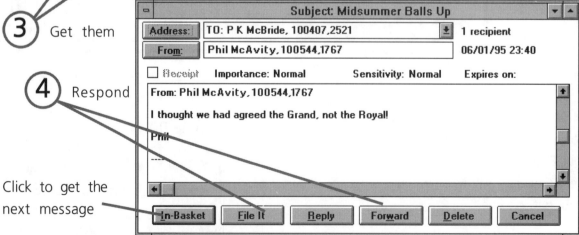

Other services

News

Games

Reference

Finance

Shopping

Travel

Before we leave CompuServe, it is worth mentioning the other services offered to its members.

- News gives access to PA News Online, Reuter UK News Clips and many other worldwide newswires.

- Games covers multi-user on-line games – keep the kids off these! – as well as libraries of games for downloading.

- Reference materials are drawn from over 850 databases including on-line versions of some major reference works, with an Encyclopedia promised early in 1995.

- Finance covers stock market quotes and sources of advice for investors.

- Shopping lets you order an increasing range of stuff – not just for computers – over the modem link.

- Travel links you to the worldwide airline booking system so that you can plan your travel arrangements, and even book tickets. (Though your local travel agent can probably do you a better deal!) The new UK accommodation and travel section includes railway timetables, AA Roadwatch, restaurants and golf club guides.

- Magazines, health, education, reviews of films, vidoes, plays and books....and much more

Summary

❏ You can **try CompuServe for free** with the Made Simple special offer!

❏ The **CompuServe Information Manager** can be downloaded, or sent for by snail mail. It will need a little configuration before you first use it.

❏ CompuServe has **local nodes** throughout the country. You may find it cheaper and easier to connect to one of these, rather than the London main node.

❏ In **WinCIM**, you can access services through the icons or by selecting from menus.

❏ There are **forums** to cover most interests and many occupations. As a forum member you have access to the forum's libraries of files and can comunicate with other members, either by mail or in on-line conferences.

❏ The **File finder** facility lets you track down files from ConpuServe's databanks.

❏ If you can't find what you want in File finder, you can use **ftp** to download files from anywhere in the Internet.

❏ **E-mail** can be composed and read on- or off-line.

❏ Compuserve offers **other information services** to its members, as well as Internet access.

6 WinNET

Starting with WinNET 84

Setting up 86

Off-line mail 88

WinNET tools 90

Newsgroup subscription 92

The news desk 94

Summary 96

Starting with WinNET

WinNET is the e-mail and Usenet News service of the PC User Group, and if what you want from the Internet is mail and news, it is probably the simplest and most effective solution around today. What makes it so easy to use are two excellent Windows software packages - WinNET Mail and WinTools.

Getting the software

Either download the software using Terminal, as shown here, or ring the PC User Group. (See the panel.)

You will have to register with them to use the service. This can also be done either by e-mail or voice phone. When registering, please state that you are an Internet Made Simple reader. Your first month's membership will cost you less than this book, and give you a chance to judge how far WinNET suits your needs.

The PC User Group

can be contacted at:
    PO Box 360, 84-88 Pinner Rd
    Harrow HA1 4LQ, England
    Tel: +44 (0)181-863 1191
    Fax: +44 (0)181-863 6095
    E-Mail: help+win-uk.net
The mail service costs £6.75 +VAT per month.
The group also offers an interactive service, with full World Wide Web connection, for £12+VAT

Basic steps

1 Open **Terminal** and make the **Settings:**

Phone: 0181 723 7300

Terminal: VT100

Communications: 8 Data, No Parity, 1 Stop bit

Baud Rate: as fast as possible up to 28800

2 Select **Phone - Dial.**

3 For the *nickname*, type **WINNET**

4 For the *password*, press **[Enter]**

5 Select **1** for the **Download** menu

6 At --More -- press the **[Spacebar]**

7 At the second list, type **h** for WNMAIL24.ZIP.

8 Select **Transfers – Receive Binary File**, and set this to save WNMAIL24.ZIP in your **temp** directory.

9 Download WNTOOLS.ZIP in the same way.

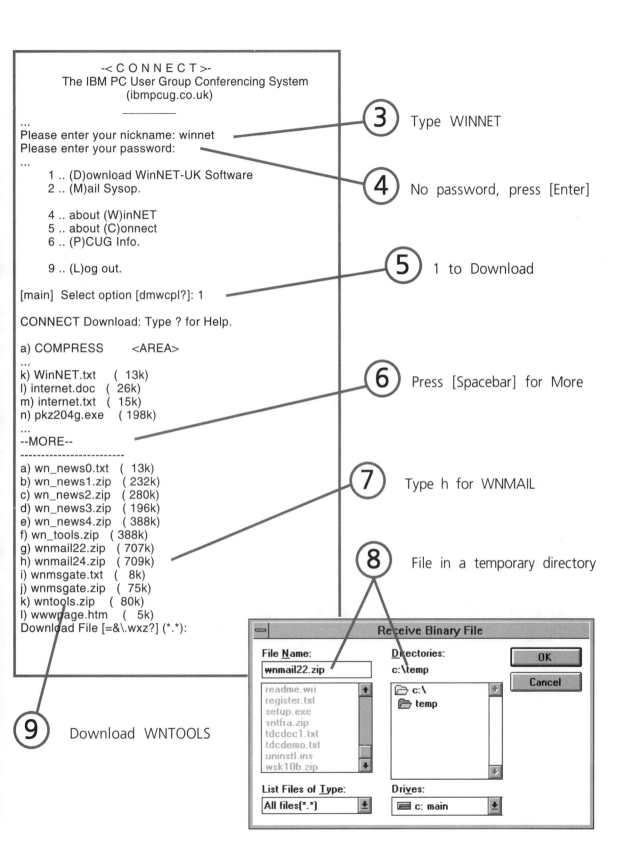

```
-<C O N N E C T>-
The IBM PC User Group Conferencing System
(ibmpcug.co.uk)
_____

...
Please enter your nickname: winnet
Please enter your password:

...
    1 .. (D)ownload WinNET-UK Software
    2 .. (M)ail Sysop.

    4 .. about (W)inNET
    5 .. about (C)onnect
    6 .. (P)CUG Info.

    9 .. (L)og out.

[main]  Select option [dmwcpl?]: 1

CONNECT Download: Type ? for Help.

a) COMPRESS      <AREA>

...
k) WinNET.txt    ( 13k)
l) internet.doc  ( 26k)
m) internet.txt  ( 15k)
n) pkz204g.exe   ( 198k)

...
--MORE--
------------------------
a) wn_news0.txt  ( 13k)
b) wn_news1.zip  ( 232k)
c) wn_news2.zip  ( 280k)
d) wn_news3.zip  ( 196k)
e) wn_news4.zip  ( 388k)
f) wn_tools.zip  ( 388k)
g) wnmail22.zip  ( 707k)
h) wnmail24.zip  ( 709k)
i) wnmsgate.txt  ( 8k)
j) wnmsgate.zip  ( 75k)
k) wntools.zip   ( 80k)
l) wwwpage.htm   ( 5k)
Download File [=&\.wxz?] (*.*):
```

(3) Type WINNET

(4) No password, press [Enter]

(5) 1 to Download

(6) Press [Spacebar] for More

(7) Type h for WNMAIL

(8) File in a temporary directory

(9) Download WNTOOLS

Receive Binary File

File Name:
wnmail22.zip

readme.wri
register.txt
setup.exe
sntfra.zip
tdcdec1.txt
tdcdemo.txt
uninstl.ins
wsk10b.zip

List Files of Type:
All files(*.*)

Directories:
c:\temp

c:\
temp

Drives:
c: main

OK
Cancel

Setting up

Unzip wnmail24.zip into your temporary subdirectory and run SETUP.EXE using the File Run command in File Manager. Unzip wn_tools.zip into a different subdirectory (e.g. \TEMP\TOOLS and then run its SETUP program from there.

When installing the **program files**, just let it run through on the default settings – it knows what it's doing. The **System Names** and **Communications** parameters do need some input fromyou.

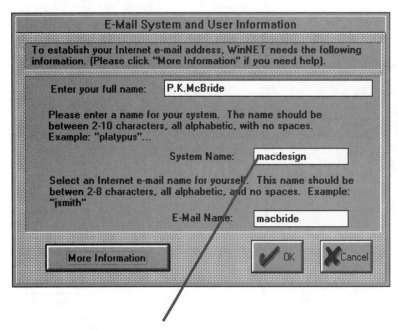

Think carefully about this. The system name is the only one you cannot change later.

Three names are required:

❑ The **full name** is what you are normally known by;

❑ the **system** name should be between 2 and 10 characters;

❑ the **e-mail** name between 3 and 8 characters.

System and e-mail names should be letters or digits only – no spaces – and are combined to form your e-mail address, in the form:

email@system.win-uk.net

Notes

- ❏ The **phone number** can include your Mercury code if appropriate

- ❏ The **Interface speed** can be set higher than your modem's baud rate, as compression pushes the effective rate up.

- ❏ Set the **CPU utilization** to Medium or High to begin with. You can adjust it later, when you have seen how it works in practice.

Take note

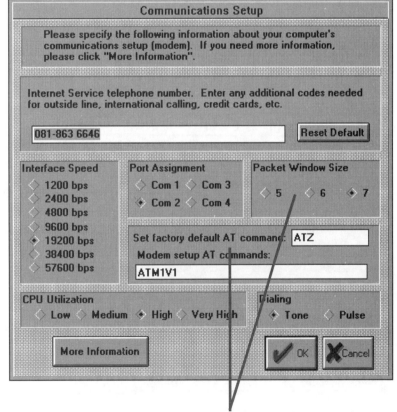

WinNET has nodes in Cambridge, Edinburgh, Manchester, Bristol and Birmingham, as well as London. If you would prefer to connect to one of these, use the Select Node option of WinTools

Communications

You should be familiar with most of what you see here – with one exception. The Call Server program (see next page) runs in the background – i.e. you can be doing other things while it gets your mail. The system needs to know how much priority to give to this. With very high **CPU utilization**, when Call Server is running, any other active programs will almost grind to a halt, but you will get your mail downloaded and filed on disk quickly. Set to low, the Call Server's activities will scarcely interrupt your other work.

Communications Setup

Please specify the following information about your computer's communications setup (modem). If you need more information, please click "More Information".

Internet Service telephone number. Enter any additional codes needed for outside line, international calling, credit cards, etc.

| 081-863 6646 | Reset Default |

Interface Speed
- ◇ 1200 bps
- ◇ 2400 bps
- ◇ 4800 bps
- ◇ 9600 bps
- ◈ 19200 bps
- ◇ 38400 bps
- ◇ 57600 bps

Port Assignment
- ◇ Com 1 ◇ Com 3
- ◈ Com 2 ◇ Com 4

Packet Window Size
- ◇ 5 ◇ 6 ◈ 7

Set factory default AT command: ATZ
Modem setup AT commands:
ATM1V1

CPU Utilization
◇ Low ◇ Medium ◈ High ◇ Very High

Dialing
◈ Tone ◇ Pulse

More Information   ✓ OK   ✗ Cancel

Leave the defaults – if they don't work, you can run Setup again and adjust them

Off-line mail

WinNET is an off-line system. You call up, once a day, to pick up your mail and news, and to send any messages you have written. If you subscribe to half a dozen or so newsgroups, and have a moderate amount of mail, your connect time should be no more than a minute or two.

The whole process is automated. All you have to do is set the Call Server running. It then sends and receives all the files, hangs up the phone, and stores the mail and newsgroup articles in the appropriate places.

② Watch files come and go

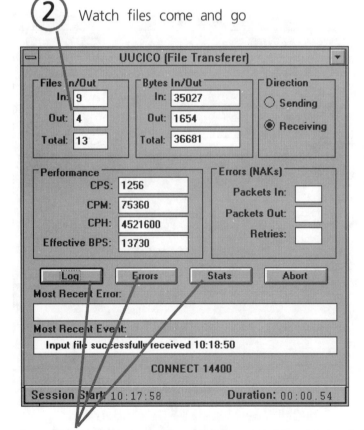

Log, Error reports or Usage Stats can be obtained from Call Server, while it is running, or from WinTools

Basic steps

1 Run the Call Server by clicking from Program Manager, or

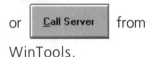 from WinNET,

or **Call Server** from WinTools.

2 Restore it from its Minimized icon and watch it while it runs, or go for a cuppa

❑ As Call Server closes down, it sets [Mail Man] running, to sort the post. When this has finished, you will see

 [New Mail] at the bottom of your screen.

3 Double click the **New Mail** icon to open up WinNET mail.

4 Read your mail.

Print current mail

Run Call Server

Open incoming mail folder

Open mail folder list

Write new mail

Reply to current mail

Forward to third party

Delete

Move to another folder

Work through list

Open Newsgroup list

Tidy display

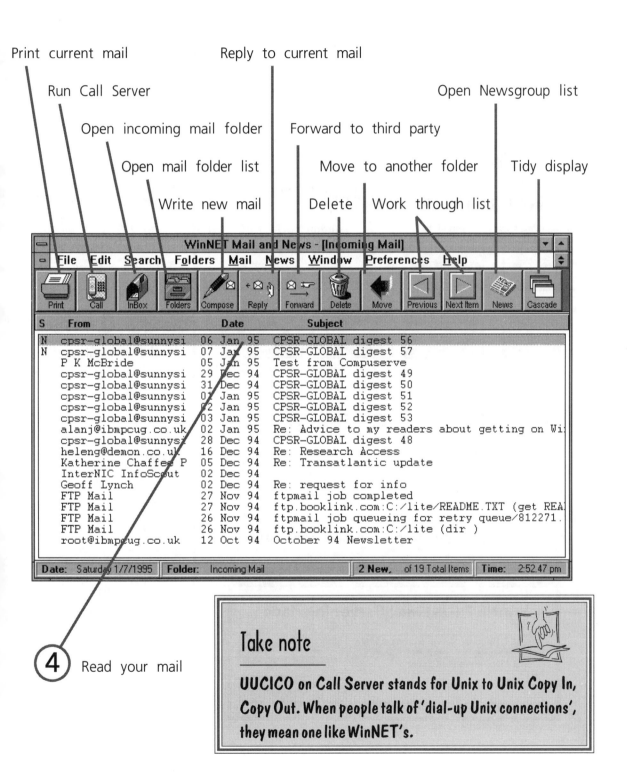

S	From	Date	Subject
N	cpsr-global@sunnysi	06 Jan 95	CPSR-GLOBAL digest 56
N	cpsr-global@sunnysi	07 Jan 95	CPSR-GLOBAL digest 57
	P K McBride	05 Jan 95	Test from Compuserve
	cpsr-global@sunnysi	29 Dec 94	CPSR-GLOBAL digest 49
	cpsr-global@sunnysi	31 Dec 94	CPSR-GLOBAL digest 50
	cpsr-global@sunnysi	01 Jan 95	CPSR-GLOBAL digest 51
	cpsr-global@sunnysi	02 Jan 95	CPSR-GLOBAL digest 52
	cpsr-global@sunnysi	03 Jan 95	CPSR-GLOBAL digest 53
	alanj@ibmpcug.co.uk	02 Jan 95	Re: Advice to my readers about getting on Wi
	cpsr-global@sunnysi	28 Dec 94	CPSR-GLOBAL digest 48
	heleng@demon.co.uk	16 Dec 94	Re: Research Access
	Katherine Chaffee P	05 Dec 94	Re: Transatlantic update
	InterNIC InfoScout	02 Dec 94	
	Geoff Lynch	02 Dec 94	Re: request for info
	FTP Mail	27 Nov 94	ftpmail job completed
	FTP Mail	27 Nov 94	ftp.booklink.com:C:/lite/README.TXT (get REA
	FTP Mail	26 Nov 94	ftpmail job queueing for retry queue/812271.
	FTP Mail	26 Nov 94	ftp.booklink.com:C:/lite (dir)
	root@ibmpcug.co.uk	12 Oct 94	October 94 Newsletter

Date: Saturday 1/7/1995   Folder: Incoming Mail   2 New, of 19 Total Items   Time: 2:52.47 pm

④ Read your mail

Take note

UUCICO on Call Server stands for Unix to Unix Copy In, Copy Out. When people talk of 'dial-up Unix connections', they mean one like WinNET's.

WinNET tools

This neat little utility gives simple access to the suite of programs that make up the WinNET system. Some of these can also be accessed directly from Program Manager; some cannot be reached any other way.

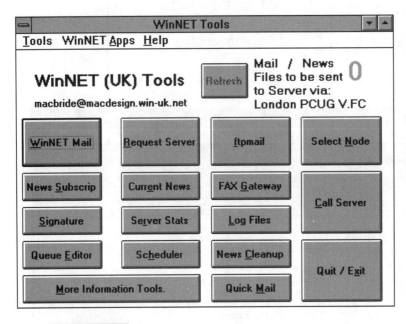

Use **Request Server** to get files, interrogate the Movie Database (a must for fans), or change your Mail List subscriptions. Each option has a dialog box for creating your requests. They can then be mailed from here.

Queue Editor lets you get into the queue of mail waiting to be sent and delete those you have thought better of.

Server Stats sends a request to WinNET to let you know how much time you have used, and what you owe them.

FAX Gateway links you to the normal phone/fax system to send a pre-written text (or Postscript) file as a fax.

Quick Mail is a simple editor/posting system for composing brief notes.

Log Files gives you access to the same error reports usage log and stats that you can see in Call Server.It also lets you delete old log files and clear some disk space.

Use 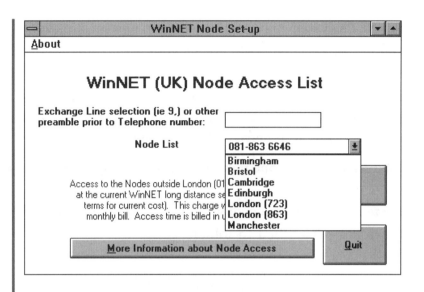 **Select Node** if there is a node near you. Note that the long-distance surcharge cuts down the saving on the phone bill.

With **Signature** you can create a short text file to add to all your mail as your personal signature. Signatures often include witty quotes or ASCII 'art' – pictures created with characters. Netiquette requires that it should be no more than four lines long.

WinNET Node Set-up

About

WinNET (UK) Node Access List

Exchange Line selection (ie 9,) or other preamble prior to Telephone number:

Node List   081-863 6646

Birmingham
Bristol
Cambridge
Edinburgh
London (723)
London (863)
Manchester

Access to the Nodes outside London (01 at the current WinNET long distance se terms for current cost). This charge w monthly bill. Access time is billed in u

More Information about Node Access   Quit

To run Call Server automatically every day, use **Scheduler** to set the dial-up times, then go to Program Manager and drag the ***D*** icon into your Startup group

Take note

Any tools not covered here are deal with in the next few pages.

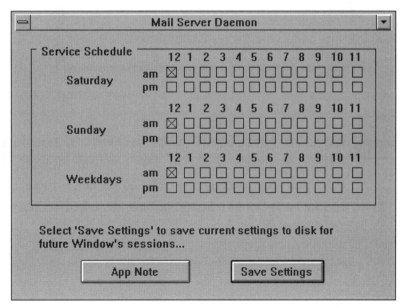

Mail Server Daemon

Service Schedule

		12 1 2 3 4 5 6 7 8 9 10 11
Saturday	am	☒ ☐ ☐ ☐ ☐ ☐ ☐ ☐ ☐ ☐ ☐ ☐
	pm	☐ ☐ ☐ ☐ ☐ ☐ ☐ ☐ ☐ ☐ ☐ ☐
Sunday	am	☒ ☐ ☐ ☐ ☐ ☐ ☐ ☐ ☐ ☐ ☐ ☐
	pm	☐ ☐ ☐ ☐ ☐ ☐ ☐ ☐ ☐ ☐ ☐ ☐
Weekdays	am	☒ ☐ ☐ ☐ ☐ ☐ ☐ ☐ ☐ ☐ ☐ ☐
	pm	☐ ☐ ☐ ☐ ☐ ☐ ☐ ☐ ☐ ☐ ☐ ☐

Select 'Save Settings' to save current settings to disk for future Window's sessions...

App Note   Save Settings

Newsgroup subscription

WinNET's system makes subscribing to newsgroups very simple. All you have to do is pick your group and tell the system you want to subscribe. It will mail a subscription request to the appropriate place and set up a **folder** to store incoming articles. When you join a newsgroup, you normally start to receive articles the next day.

Unsubscribing is done in much the same way. Note that when you leave a group, its articles generally continue to come through for a few days. These are collected in the **News not subscribed to** folder.

```
┌─────────────────────────────────────────┬───┬───┐
│ ═    │      Usenet News Group Folders    │ ▼ │ ▲ │
├──────┴───────────────────────────────────┴───┴───┤
│ #New      News Group Name                        │
├──────────────────────────────────────────────────┤
│   16    comp.internet.net-happenings             │
│  173    comp.unix.questions                      │
│   30    news.not.subscribed.to                   │
│   13    sci.physics.fusion                       │
│    1    rec.humor.funny                          │
│   17    uk.net                                   │
│    6    uk.sources                               │
│                                                  │
└──────────────────────────────────────────────────┘
```

opens the News Group Folder list. Clicking on a folder name then opens it. The numbers in the list show how many new (unread) articles there are in each folder. Some groups generate more articles than others.

Basic steps

❑ **Subscribing**

1 Open WnTools and select `News Subscrip`

2 Drop down the list of categories under **Which News Group to Search for?**

3 Pick a category and click `Search`

4 Scroll through the resulting list to see what's there.

5 If you find a news group that looks interesting, select it and click `Subscribe`

5 Repeat steps 2 to 5 as wanted, then Quit.

❑ Your subscription requests will be posted next time you use Call Server.

Basic steps

❑ **Unsubscribing**

1 Open the News Sub-
scription panel as
shown on the left

2 Select the newsgroup
from the list in the
right hand pane

3 Click [Unsubscribe]

② Pick a category

③ Start the search

⑤ Subscribe

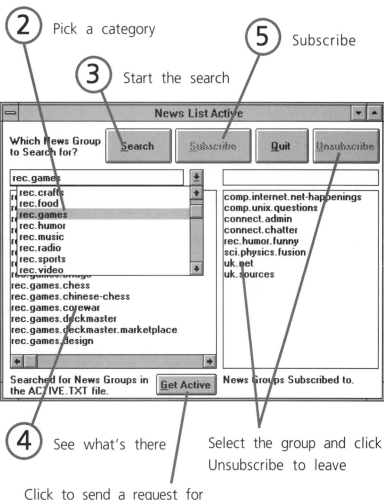

④ See what's there

Click to send a request for
the latest list of newsgroups

Select the group and click
Unsubscribe to leave

Take note

**Mailing lists are handled through the e-mail system. To
subscribe to a list you usually send e-mail to:**

listserv@sunnyside.com

with the message

SUBSCRIBE listname your name your e-mail address

The news desk

If people are using the Subject line properly, you can see at a glance whether or not you want to read the article. Having read it, you can respond in several ways.

Copies the article to another folder, where it will not be deleted when you do a cleanup. (See opposite page)

Print a copy on paper

Respond to the author only.

Submit an article to the group – be relevant and brief.

```
WinNET Mail and News - [comp.unix.questions]

File   Edit   Search   Folders   Mail   News   Window   Preferences   Help

Print   Call   InBox   Reply   Forward   Post   FollowUp   Copy   Mark   Previous   Next Item   News   Cascade

S  Ln     From              Date        Subject
N  21   Kirk Rafferty       05 Jan   Re: Moving *ALL* files from a subdirectory
N  24   Mark A. Bialik      05 Jan   Help! X11/Xterm disable functions
N  20   Dr.F.Mencaraglia    05 Jan   raw writing to disk: which sectors must be
N  14   CREIGH KELLEY       05 Jan   Re: Using UNIX
N  8    Shobhik Chaudhuri   05 Jan   WWW homepage <---> UNIX commands
N  1    Douglas Wong        05 Jan   Deleting file called -F
N  26   Ananda M. Kar       05 Jan   Re: WWW homepage <---> UNIX commands
N  69   Brian Aitken        05 Jan   Re: Newsgroup reading list suggestions wa
N  28   Frank Obits         07 Jan   Re: Newsgroup reading list suggestions wa
N  13   patrick             06 Jan   Re: Newsgroup reading list suggestions wa
N  22   Nuno Serrenho       07 Jan   Re: Newsgroup reading list suggestions wa
N  51   Thomas Schreiber    05 Jan   interactive rsh and interrupts
N  31   Sea-Hawon Choi      05 Jan   Q: Demon process
N  10   Aaron Barnett       05 Jan   vi g/foo/p
N  25   Bart Lamiroy        05 Jan   Creating new versions with SCCS
N  33   Mehtap Kologlu      05 Jan   Re: Allowing all addresses with sendmail
```

```
* ------ News Composition Editor ------ *

NewsGroup(s):  comp.unix.questions

Followup-To:                                    Edit    Done    Cancel

Subject:       Re: Using UNIX

In article <3ev641$oo5@ixnews3.ix.netcom.com>, CREIGH KELLEY (
>I am a long time DOS user who is trying to learn UNIX. I have
>several books on the subject but can't find a system to pract
>Any suggestions?
>
This year Linux seems to be the No 1 choice for Unix on a PC –
is available as freeware over the Net. |

Date:  Thursday 1/12/1995   NEWS PREPARATION            Time:   9.40.48 am
```

Copies the article into your editor, tacking **Re:** to the subject line. Edit it and add comments, before posting.

Basic steps

1
Click **News Cleanup** in

WinTools, or 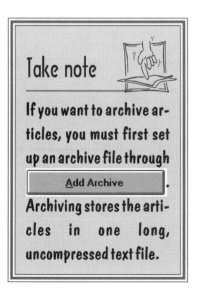 News Cleanup

in Program Manager

2
Set the age limit for the cleanup.

3
Decide whether you want **Cleanup** and/or **Archive**

4
Click **START**

If there are a lot of old articles to shift, go and have a cup of tea.

Take note

If you want to archive articles, you must first set up an archive file through **Add Archive** .

Archiving stores the articles in one long, uncompressed text file.

Cleaning up

One of the problems of belonging to newsgroups is the amount of storage space required. The half dozen groups that I subscribe to, generate a Megabyte of files each week – and only one of these has heavy traffic. Join *alt.tv.xfiles* or *alt.startrek* (one of 12 Star Trek newsgroups) or any other group that attracts large numbers of articulate enthusiasts, and you will soon be wondering where all your hard disk went. Fortunately there is a Cleanup program that removes old articles.

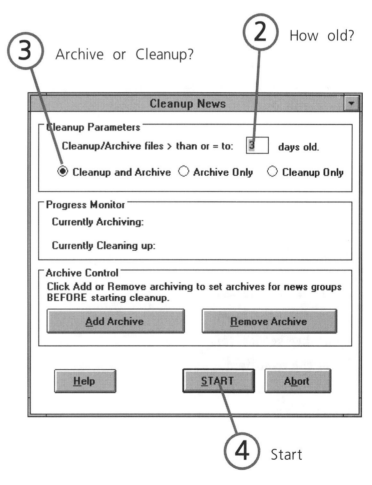

③ Archive or Cleanup?   **②** How old?

④ Start

Cleanup News

Cleanup Parameters
Cleanup/Archive files > than or = to: 3   days old.

● Cleanup and Archive   ○ Archive Only   ○ Cleanup Only

Progress Monitor
Currently Archiving:
Currently Cleaning up:

Archive Control
Click Add or Remove archiving to set archives for news groups BEFORE starting cleanup.

Add Archive   **Remove Archive**

Help   **START**   **Abort**

Summary

❑ **WinNET** is an off-line mail-based service run by the PC Users Group.

❑ WinNET **Mail** and **Tools** are efficient and well-designed programs that make it easy to get the best out of the system.

❑ The **Call Server** can be set to run automatically at a chosen time each day, or you can call up as and when you need to.

❑ You can access the USENET and other **newsgroups** through WinNET.

❑ There are simple facilities for subscribing to newsgroups, and for archiving or removing old news articles.

Take note

The PC User Group also offers **CONNECT**, an interactive service, for those who want ftp direct or access to the World Wide Web.

7 Trumpet Winsock

Local links to the World 98

Trumpet Winsock 99

Getting on-line 101

Archie file locator 102

ftp the easy way 104

Gopher it 106

Eudora mail 108

Summary 110

Local links to the World

CompuServe and the PC User Group are only two of the many organisations, large and small, providing access to the Internet. The smaller firms initially served only their local area, though an increasing number now also have a national network of nodes. Small providers can sometimes be an excellent choice, offering a more personal service and high level of support, but the quality is variable. Growth rates are high, and not all firms expand their hardware and phone connections fast enough. Trying to get on-line through such a firm can be frustrating.

TCP (Total Connectivity Providers) is an example of a small service which can be reached through a national network of nodes. It provides full and easy access to the World Wide Web, interactive ftp (for getting files), archie (for finding them), plus an e-mail system – all in Windows packages. The programs they supply are all standard shareware or freeware. All TCP does is what any good service should do – they configure the software so that it is ready for you to use, and they bundle it into one neat, self-installing package.

1 Contact TCP (details below) and sign up. They will set up your account and send you a disk and brief manual.

2 When you get the disk, go into Windows and run the INSTALL program from File Manager. You will need about 3.5 Mb of disk space.

3 Accept their suggestions at the prompts and in a few minutes you will have a new program group.

Take note

TCP more commonly stands for Transfer Control Protocol and is the basis of interactive access over the Internet.

Free Trial Offer

Mention 'The Internet Made Simple' when you join and TCP will waive the initial set-up fees, and give you one month's free trial subscription.

TCP is at: PO Box 454, Southampton, SO16 3WR

Tel: 01703-393392

E-mail: sales @ tcp.co.uk

Trumpet Winsock

1 Run the TCP program – it calls itself Trumpet Winsock when it opens

2 Open the File menu and select Setup.

3 Type in your IP address and that of your server.

4 The SLIP port is your COM port – 1 or 2.

5 Set the Baud rate.

6 Make sure the Internal SLIP, Hardware Handshake and Van Jacobson compression boxes are all checked.

7 Click OK.

This is the TCP (Transfer Control Protocol) communications manager that controls your connection through to the Internet. Set it up correctly, and everything flows smoothly. It needs to know your IP address and that of your name server (your provider will supply these), as well as basic modem details.

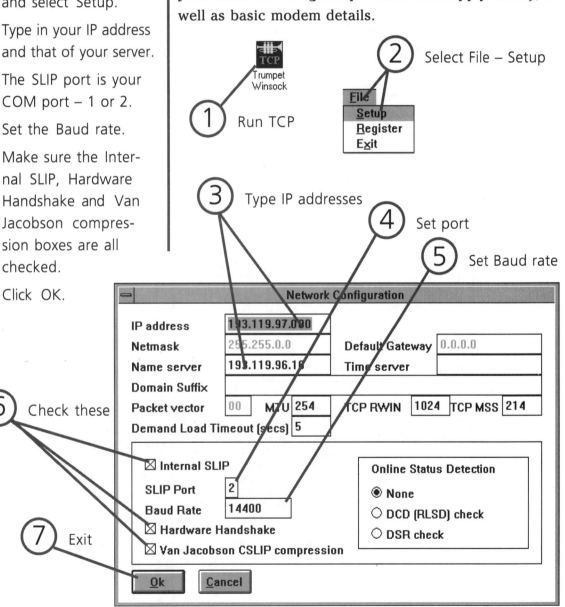

99

Editing the Login script

Like most comms software, Winsock can run a login script – a file of commands, to save you having to type the phone number, your ID and password whenever you want to get on-line. This must be edited to give it your details.

● If you are using Winsock with a system other than TCP, and no basic script has been provided, follow the pattern shown here, and save it as *login.cmd*.

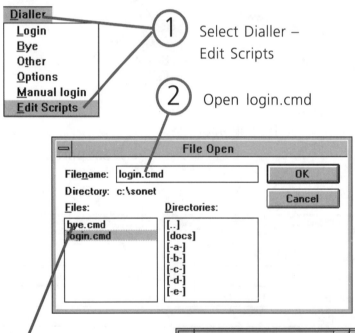

The bye.cmd script, to logout, normally reads:

    sleep 3
    output +++
    sleep 3
    output ath0\r

1 Select Dialler – Edit Scripts from Trumpet Winsock's menus.

2 Open login.cmd. This will take you into Notepad for editing.

3 Replace:

<telno> with the your provider's number.

<name> with your user name. It will probably need -slip or -pop at the end – check your paperwork.

<password> with the password you have been given.

4 Save and exit back to Winsock.

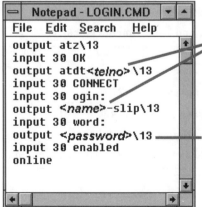

③ Type in your details

\13 is the code equivalent of pressing [Enter]

Basic steps

1 Run TCP (Winsock)

2 Open the Dialler menu and select Login

3 Watch the script run through and make sure all is well.

4 Once you have the Packet mode enabled message, click the Minimize button.

❑ You are ready to run a user program.

Whichever of the user programs – ftp, gopher, mail or web browser – you want to use, you must first run Winsock and login. The comms manager can then be minimised out of the way and forgotten about until you have finished your session.

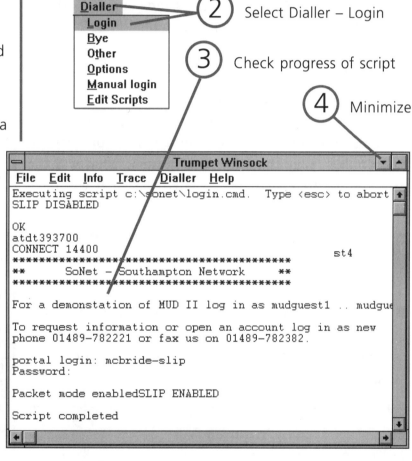

② Select Dialler – Login

③ Check progress of script

④ Minimize

Close it down when you have finished.

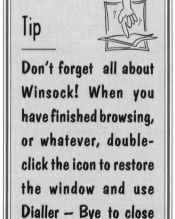

Tip

Don't forget all about Winsock! When you have finished browsing, or whatever, double-click the icon to restore the window and use Dialler – Bye to close down the connection.

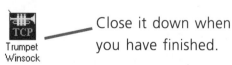

Archie file locator

ARCHIE
Network File
Locator

You can use ftp to browse through remote databanks to see what's there, but it's a slow way to find files. Far better to get Archie to track them down for you. To use it, you have to connect to an Archie server – preferably your nearest – and give it part of, or the whole, name of the file you want to find. The Archie program at the server will then search the Internet's archives and come up with the URL's (locations and names) of matching files.

Substring searches

It is quite likely that you will not know the exact name of the file. For example, if you may come across MPEG files – videos for computers – and want an MPEG program so that you can play them on your system. What will the program file be called? It is a fair bet that it will have MPEG in the name.

● Don't use wildcards. This is not DOS. Give the bit you know (or guess). If there is a file that contains it anywhere in the name, it will be matched.

● Do be as complete as you can. The shorter the substring, the longer the search. Archie estimated it would take 30 minutes to find all MPEG matches – I aborted at that point!

Take note

Giving the exact name makes the search simpler and quicker. Restricting the search to a domain also speeds things up. If an exact, restricted search fails, you can try a wider one later.

1 Use Winsock to login.

2 Run **Archie**.

3 Enter the name – or part of the name – of the file to **Search** for.

4 Click **Exact** if you gave the whole name; **Substring**, if you gave only a part.

5 Select an **Archie server** from the list, trying the closest first.

6 If you want to restrict the search to the UK, type *uk* in the **Domain** slot.

7 Click ⬛Search⬛ to start.

8 Give it a moment to locate the host, then check the **Status Bar**.

9 If there is a long **Queue** of other users, click ⬛Abort⬛, select a new server and try again there.

❑ If you are successful, you will see a list of file details.

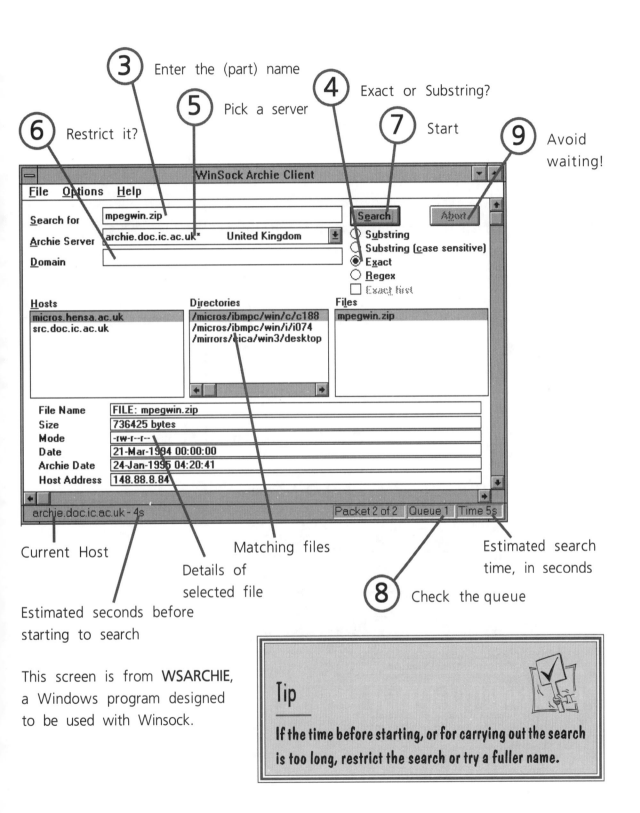

③ Enter the (part) name

⑤ Pick a server

④ Exact or Substring?

⑥ Restrict it?

⑦ Start

⑨ Avoid waiting!

WinSock Archie Client

File   Options   Help

Search for   mpegwin.zip   Search   Abort

Archie Server   archie.doc.ic.ac.uk*   United Kingdom   ○ Substring
                                                               ○ Substring (case sensitive)
Domain   ● Exact
                                                               ○ Regex
                                                               □ Exact first

Hosts   Directories   Files
micros.hensa.ac.uk   /micros/ibmpc/win/c/c188   mpegwin.zip
src.doc.ic.ac.uk   /micros/ibmpc/win/i/i074
                          /mirrors/cica/win3/desktop

File Name   FILE: mpegwin.zip
Size   736425 bytes
Mode   -rw-r--r--
Date   21-Mar-1994 00:00:00
Archie Date 24-Jan-1995 04:20:41
Host Address 148.88.8.84

archie.doc.ic.ac.uk - 4s   Packet 2 of 2   Queue 1   Time 5s

Current Host

Matching files

Details of selected file

Estimated search time, in seconds

⑧ Check the queue

Estimated seconds before starting to search

This screen is from **WSARCHIE**, a Windows program designed to be used with Winsock.

> **Tip**
>
> If the time before starting, or for carrying out the search is too long, restrict the search or try a fuller name.

103

ftp the easy way

FTP
File Transfer
Program

WS_FTP.EXE is a Windows program for use with Winsock, and offers probably the simplest way to do ftp. You tell it where you want to go, and what directory to start at, then send it off to make the connection. A few points to note:

● You must login through Winsock first.

● You must know exactly the host name.

● If you know the path to the directory, it speeds things up. If you do not give it, you will start at the top of the directory structure and can work your way down.

● You won't always get through – the site may be off-line, or already crowded with other ftp'ers. Try later.

● All ftp URL references take the form:
    ftp://host.name/path/to/directory/filename
    Use the information to set up your connection.

Basic steps

1 Run FTP.

2 Pull down the Profile list and pick a site.

or

   Create a profile for a new site. Click **New** and enter a profile name and the exact Host name.

3 Make sure that **Anonymous login** in checked. This sets the **User ID** to *Anonymous* and that the **Password** to your user ID.

4 Enter the directory path on the **Remote Host**, if known.

5 Click **Save** if you have set up a new profile, or made changes that you want to keep.

6 Click **OK** to start the connection.

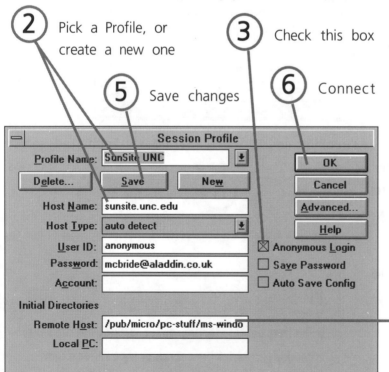

② Pick a Profile, or create a new one

③ Check this box

⑤ Save changes

⑥ Connect

④ Set the Directory

Basic steps

1 Change directory if need be – use the same techniques as in any File Manager.

2 Highlight a file that interests you.

3 Opt for **ASCII** to transfer text files, **Binary** for any others.

4 Set the directory on your local system to receive a file.

5 Click [←] to download.

6 Use [Close] to return to the first panel and set up a new session.

7 Click [Exit] to end.

Using the ftp connection

Ftp gives you a two-way, interactive connection to the remote host. You can treat its directories and files as if they were in a drive in your own machine – almost.

● Downloading is like copying a file from another disk – but much slower. Be patient.

● If you want to upload a file, only do so into a directory that welcomes contributions – if you can't see one called UPLOADS, they probably don't want your files.

● Don'tdelete or edit files or directories on the Host – it shouldn't let you, but it might have let its guard slip.

● View any README or similar files . They can be useful.

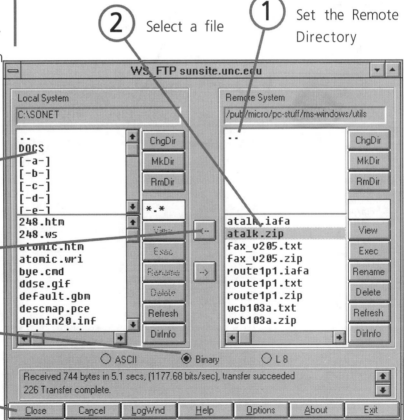

② Select a file

① Set the Remote Directory

④ Set the Local Directory

⑤ Download

③ ASCII or Binary

⑥ New host

Gopher it

Gopher Client

Hgopher is a freeware Windows gopher program for Winsock users. Some service providers do not include this in the software package, but it can be easily downloaded from an ftp site.

Gopher items include text, graphics and sounds, and Hgopher needs to know what software to use to view these. It will have found some viewers on installation; others you must tell it about. The list can be added to at any time.

1 Without starting Winsock, run Gopher, and ignore the *No connection* message.

2 Select Options – Viewer Set up.

3 In the Select View type list, pick a type that can be used by software on your system.

4 If Viewer is empty, type in the path and filename ending with %f, (to stand for the name of the data file) then click [Accept]

5 Repeat 3 and 4 for all the types you can use, then click [Done]

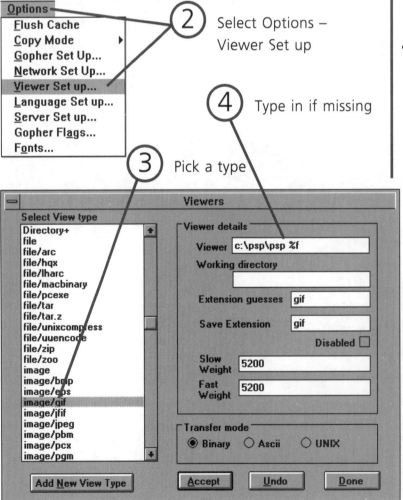

② Select Options – Viewer Set up

④ Type in if missing

③ Pick a type

Take note

As Gopher does a good job of installing itself, you should find that many of the viewers are already set up correctly

Basic steps

Gophering

1 Login through Winsock and run Gopher.

2 Open the **Commands** menu and select **Go Home**, to take you to your gopher server.

3 Click on an item name to select it. This will take you to another menu or run a viewer so that you can read/view/hear the file.

4 To save items for future reference, open the **Commands** menu and select **Save As**

All you really need to know to start exploring gopherspace, is that clicking a menu item's name selects that item. Finding the parts that interest you is another matter – but just keep following the trails through the menus. They will take you there.

● When you find sites that you want to return to in future, add them to your **Bookmark** list and you will be able to jump straight to them next time.

● As you gain experience, you might like to start investigating the **Options** to tweak the screen displays and your interaction with gopher.

Click on the name to select

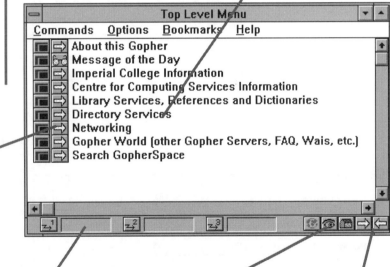

Click for info – the URL of the item

You can have up to three open links at a time. Counters show the progress of incoming data.

Toggle between view and file-saving modes

Backwards and forwards through open menus

Eudora mail

Electronic Mail

This is a freeware Winsock mail program, that can be used on- or off-line. It offers no Help, but is straightforward to use. There is a comprehensive set of commands and a small but sufficient set of icons. Customising is simple, with a clearly laid out configuration dialog box, and a set of check box switches to cover most options.

One of Eudora's attractive features is its simple means of attaching text or binary files to messages for transmission through the mail.

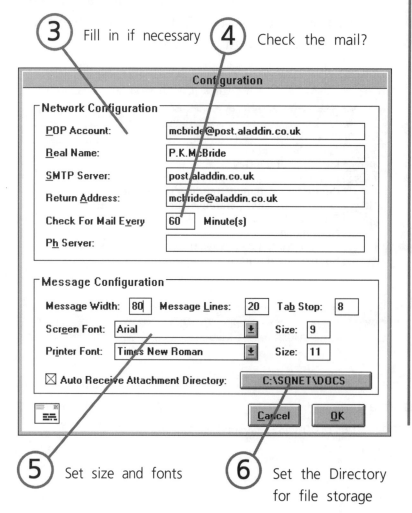

Basic steps

1 If the network configuration has not been done by your suppliers, get the details from them.

2 Open the **Special** menu and select **Configuration**.

3 Fill in the **Network configuration** details if necessary.

4 If you will be on-line for long stretches of time and want Eudora to check your mail regularly, set the interval.

5 Set the width and depth of your message area and choose fonts for the screen and printer output.

6 If you want to change the directory in which to store incoming attached files, click on the Directory button.

Mail is stored in three folders – incoming and outgoing mail, plus a trash can. Deleting a message sends it first to the trash can, which you empty when you will.

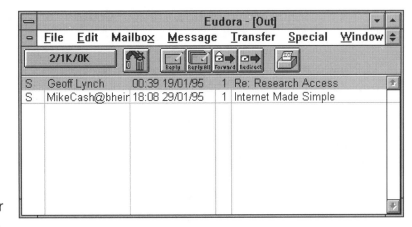

To send a graphic or other binary file, all you have to do is use the **Message – Attach Document** command and pick the file. The person you are sending it to should also have Eudora or a suitable converter.

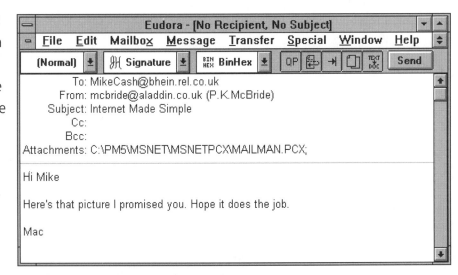

Take note

To use Eudora, you must have a POP (Point-Of-Presence) account. Note that your account name will be different from your e-mail name/address.

Summary

❑ TCP is a good example of how service providers should work.

❑ TCP gives a fully interactive connection to the Internet.

❑ The supplied software includes all the necessary tools, all of which have had the key settings configured for you.

❑ The Archie file locator provides an easy way to find files, wherever they may be on the Internet.

❑ WS_FTP is simple to use, yet quick and efficient.

❑ The Windows-based gopher software rquires little configuration before it is ready to use. Additional viewers can be added at any time, as needed.

❑ Eudora is an on- or off-line mail package, with a neat facility for attaching binary files to messages.

❑ All of the tools have a huge range of features and facilities that will keep the most advanced users happy, but can also be used easily by a novice.

8 The World Wide Web

Netscape 112

Netscape options 114

Net Directories 116

WWW URL's 118

Bookmarks 120

Hypertext 122

Summary .124

Netscape

At the time of writing, Mosaic Netscape is the newest, and probably the best, Web browser. It is quick and efficient, and though it has all the advanced features an experienced browser could want, it is simple to use.

As well as managing the hypertext links between pages, Netscape:

- can display graphics in JPEG and GIF formats, whether stored on disk or found on the Web

- gives you access to Internet newsgroups, allowing immediate downloading of the current crop of articles in any group. This is a convenient way to get the flavour of a group when you are deciding whether or not to become a subscriber.

- can be used to link to ftp sites to download files. If you know the file's name and location, it is quicker and simpler to use a dedicated ftp program like WS-FTP, but the Netscape approach is good for browsing directories and downloading.

- can link into the Gopher system. As with ftp, dedicated gopher software will do the job better, but it is handy to have the facilities within one package.

Netscape opens at its **Home** page. The default will probably be your service provider's, but you can set your own start point.

Back/forward through loaded pages

Undo

Go to Home page

Load images

Open location

Stop loading incoming page

Current location

Find

Directory buttons

Toolbar

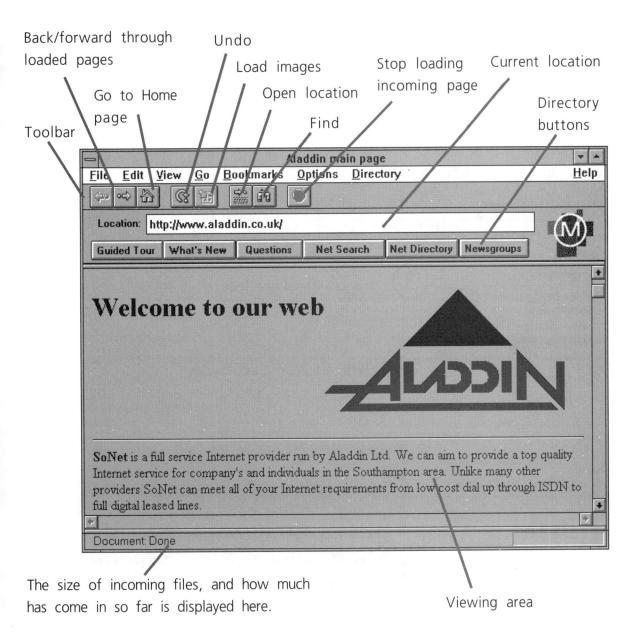

The size of incoming files, and how much has come in so far is displayed here.

Viewing area

Netscape options

You can run on the default settings at first, though there may be a few aspects you might like to configure.

The Toolbar, Location slot and Directory (and other) buttons can all be turned off, if you want a larger viewing area. The remaining menu commands will still give you full control.

Auto Loading of images can be a nuisance. Many images are purely decorative, but the size of the files greatly imcreases the time it takes to complete a connection. If you think you may be missing something, you can always load them after you have connected.

1 Open the **Options** menu

2 Turn off **Auto Load Images** for faster connections. You will then get wherever an image would appear.

3 Click to remove the tick by any of the **Show..** items you want to turn off.

4 **Save** your Options settings

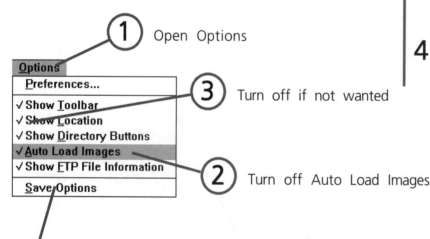

① Open Options

Options

Preferences...

√ Show <u>T</u>oolbar
√ Show <u>L</u>ocation
√ Show <u>D</u>irectory Buttons
√ <u>A</u>uto Load Images
√ Show <u>F</u>TP File Information

<u>S</u>ave Options

③ Turn off if not wanted

② Turn off Auto Load Images

④ Save your settings

Take note

The Netscape Help pages are on-line! You must be connected and have Netscape running before you can get to them. Once you are there, you can save the pages, so that you have them at hand when you are off-line

Basic steps

1 Open the **Options** menu

2 Select **Preferences**

3 Pull down the list of panels and choose **Helper Applications**

4 Work through the list and stop at any file type for which you have a suitable viewer, but which is not already handled by Netscape.

5 Type the path and filename of the viewer program, or select it through **Browse**.

❑ Check the directory preference panel, but leave the other settings at their defaults.

Take note

You can opt to save files for later viewing, or launch the application to view while on-line.

Adding viewers

Netscape's built-in viewers can display much of the incoming data, but there is a wide range file types out there on the Web. The more you can handle, the more you can see – and hear.

Check through the file type list in the Helper Applications panel, to see if there are any that you know you can handle with software already on your system. You may also spot some that you would like to be able to view. If there are, you can always track down suitable viewers in the Internet's databanks and add them later.

③ Choose Helper Applications

④ Select a type

⑤ Give the viewer

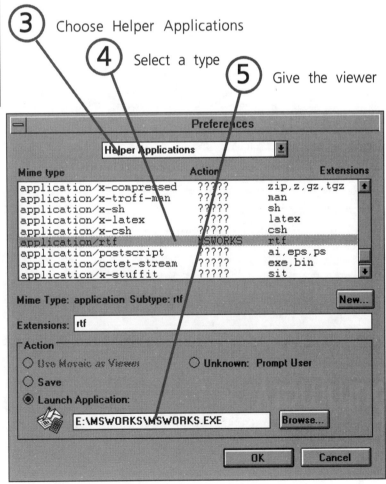

Net Directories

One of the biggest problems on the World Wide Web is finding your way round its thousands of pages. Fortunately, several organisations have produced directories that provide mapped routes into the Web. The Net Directory button takes you to the *Directory of Directories*, which offer 10 different starting points into the Web.

- The **Subject** directories have the widest coverage. Of these, the *Whole Internet Catalog* is most complete, but *Yahoo* (see opposite) is most fun.

- The **Commercial** directories are growing fast, but from a small base.

- The **Server** directories are best for ftp work.

Basic steps

1 Get on-line and run Netscape

2 Click **Net Directory** and wait for the page to load.

3 Scroll through and select a directory by clicking on its name.

② Click to load

③ Select a directory

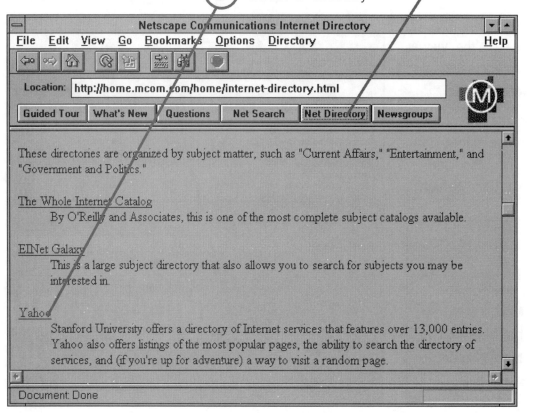

Yahoo

Yahoo is run from Stanford University in the US. At the time of writing it held links to over 29,000 pages, with more being added every day. It has a comprehensive subject catalog, as well as:

● **What's New?** to keep you abreast of the latest;

● **What's Cool?** including the not-to-be-missed *Interesting Devices connected to the Web*;

● **What's Popular?** and don't be surprised if you can't get through to these pages through overcrowding;

● **A Random Link**, which is often worth a look, just to get an idea of the range of things that are out there.

The numbers beside each heading show how many pages are linked from there. You will see that all those in the screenshot have NEW beside them – it is rare to find an area where new pages have not been added in the last few days.

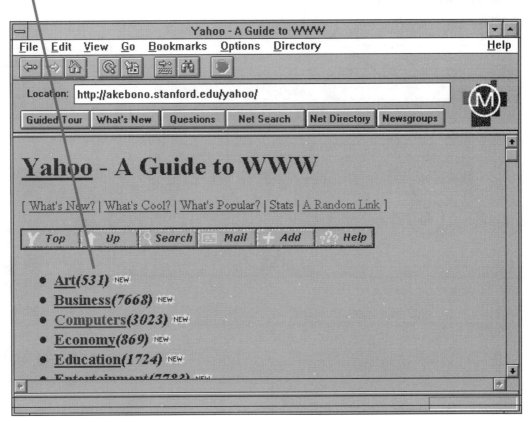

WWW URL's

Don't you just love the TIA's? (Three Letter Acronyms) The World Wide Web Uniform Resource Locators give the locations of pages. As the Web is so vast, being able to jump to a specific page is a great boon – and it is easy with Netscape. Let's see what on the BBC. Its URL is:

http://www.bbcnc.org.uk

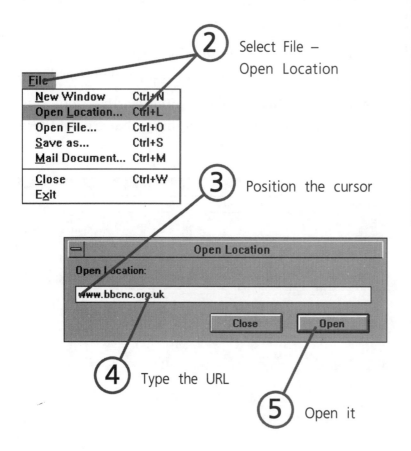

② Select File –
Open Location

③ Position the cursor

④ Type the URL

⑤ Open it

1 Make sure you have the URL to hand – they are not things that you can easily remember accurately!

2 Open the **File** menu and select **Open Location**

3 Click into the slot to place the text cursor there – it doesn't go there automatically.

4 Type in the URL, but not the *http://* prefix

5 Click [Open] and sit back and wait.

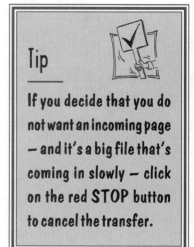

Tip

If you decide that you do not want an incoming page – and it's a big file that's coming in slowly – click on the red STOP button to cancel the transfer.

The Location slot shows the URL   Click the button to cancel a transfer

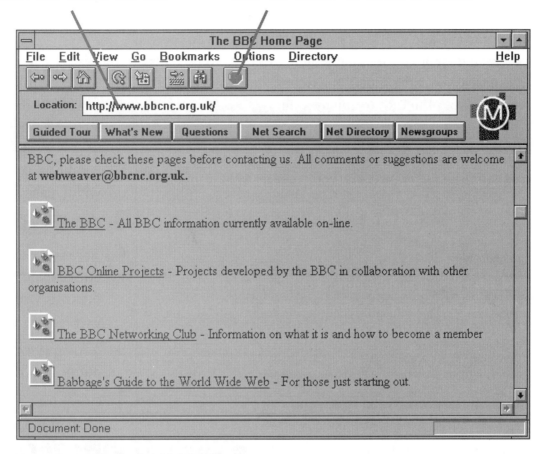

A shot from one of my favourite sites, the San Diego Bay Camera:
http://www.cts.com/~jtara/baycam.html

Late on a cold winter's evening, it's good to see the sun on the water.

Bookmarks

When you do find a good site that you want to revisit often, rather than write down its URL, to retype it back in later, you can add it to your Bookmarks. It is stored there as a recognisable page name. When you want to go back to the site, you simply pull down the list and click on its name, leaving the URL to the system.

One small, but crucial, detail – Netscape does not retain the Bookmarks when it closes. If you want to keep them from one session to the next, you must save them as a file.

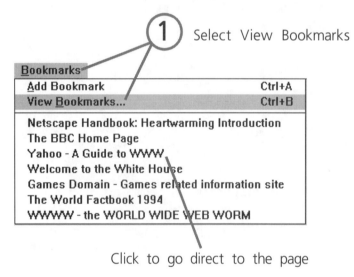

Select View Bookmarks

Click to go direct to the page

Take note

You can have any number of different sets of Bookmarks, each saved as a separate file. This is particularly useful if you are researching several distinct areas. Stick all your Bookmarks in one file, and the list could become impracticably long.

Basic steps

❏ **Saving Bookmarks**

1 Open the **Bookmarks** menu and select **View Bookmarks.**

2 A narrow Bookmark List panel will open. Click the **Edit >>** button to get the full-width panel.

3 Click **Export Bookmarks**

4 At the dialog box, give the directory and filename (with an htm extension).

❏ **Adding the current page**

1 Open the **Bookmarks** menu and click **Add Bookmark.**

That's it!

❏ **Going to a Bookmark**

1 Open the **Bookmarks** menu and click on the desired page name in the list.

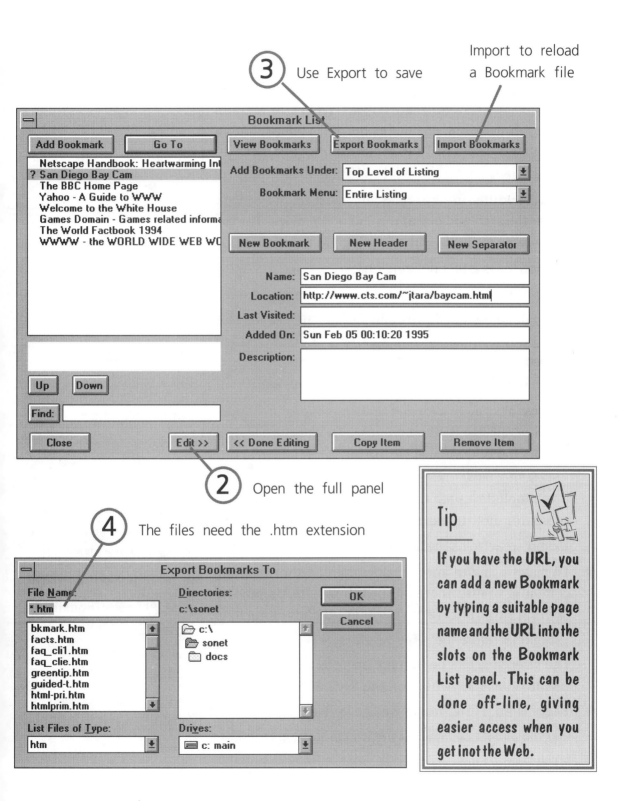

③ Use Export to save

Import to reload a Bookmark file

Bookmark List

| Add Bookmark | Go To | | View Bookmarks | Export Bookmarks | Import Bookmarks |

Netscape Handbook: Heartwarming Int
? San Diego Bay Cam
The BBC Home Page
Yahoo - A Guide to WWW
Welcome to the White House
Games Domain - Games related inform
The World Factbook 1994
WWWW - the WORLD WIDE WEB WO

Add Bookmarks Under: Top Level of Listing
Bookmark Menu: Entire Listing

New Bookmark   New Header   New Separator

Name: San Diego Bay Cam
Location: http://www.cts.com/~jtara/baycam.html
Last Visited:
Added On: Sun Feb 05 00:10:20 1995
Description:

Up   Down

Find:

Close   Edit >>   << Done Editing   Copy Item   Remove Item

② Open the full panel

④ The files need the .htm extension

Export Bookmarks To

File Name:
*.htm

bkmark.htm
facts.htm
faq_cli1.htm
faq_clie.htm
greentip.htm
guided-t.htm
html-pri.htm
htmlprim.htm

Directories:
c:\sonet

📁 c:\
📁 sonet
📁 docs

OK
Cancel

List Files of Type:
htm

Drives:
💾 c: main

Tip

If you have the URL, you can add a new Bookmark by typing a suitable page name and the URL into the slots on the Bookmark List panel. This can be done off-line, giving easier access when you get inot the Web.

Hypertext

If, as Aladdin does, your service provider offers you a free Web page, and you would like to take advantage of it, you will need to know how to create HTML (HyperText Markup Language) documents. It is not as hard as you may think. The documents are written as text files, with tags to indicate text styles and to link to other pages or files.

- Tags are written in <brackets>, and most are paired with one at the start and one at the end of the block. The tag is the same for both, with a leading / at the end. e.g.

    <h1>This is a first heading</h1>

- New paragraphs are marked by a <p> at the start only.

- Every document has two main blocks, the <head> and the <body>. The head block carries a <title>, which will be used in its Bookmark.

- The document must be enclosed in <html> tags.

- Images must be in a format that Netscape can handle – JPG or GIF are the commonest. To insert an image, give its file reference in the form:

    <img src="filename">

    If you include a path to the file, use the Unix / as the separator, not the normal DOS \ backslash. e.g.

    <img src = "/pics/mypic.jpg"

- To make a link to another document, either on your computer or elsewhere on the Internet, you anchor a reference to a phrase in your text. Anchors look like:

    <A href="reference">Key words</a>

    The reference can be to a file on your system, or the URL of a page anywhere on the Web.

- There is an HTML primer on the Web at:

    http://www.ncsa.uiuc.edu/General/Internet/WWW/HTMLPrimer.html

Tags

<html> at start and end of document

<head> around title area

<title> Bookmark title

<body> at start and end of main text

<h1> First level head

<h2> Second level head

<h3> Third sub-head

<strong> Bold

<p> new paragraph

<hr> Line spacer

 Clear break

Take note

The pages you will see on the Internet all have the extension .HTML, which is four letters. The Unix systems that run the Internet can handle long filenames and extensions – DOS can't. Save files with the extension .HTM. Netscape recognises this.

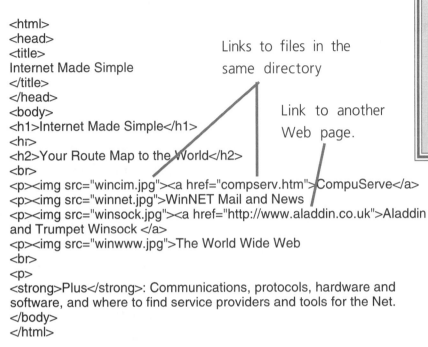

```
<html>
<head>
<title>
Internet Made Simple
</title>
</head>
<body>
<h1>Internet Made Simple</h1>
<hr>
<h2>Your Route Map to the World</h2>
<br>
<p><img src="wincim.jpg"><a href="compserv.htm">CompuServe</a>
<p><img src="winnet.jpg">WinNET Mail and News
<p><img src="winsock.jpg"><a href="http://www.aladdin.co.uk">Aladdin
and Trumpet Winsock </a>
<p><img src="winwww.jpg">The World Wide Web
<br>
<p>
<strong>Plus</strong>: Communications, protocols, hardware and
software, and where to find service providers and tools for the Net.
</body>
</html>
```

Links to files in the same directory

Link to another Web page.

Tip

To see how your HTML document looks, run Netscape and load it in with File – Open File.

To see how the tags work, compare this original text with the formatted display.

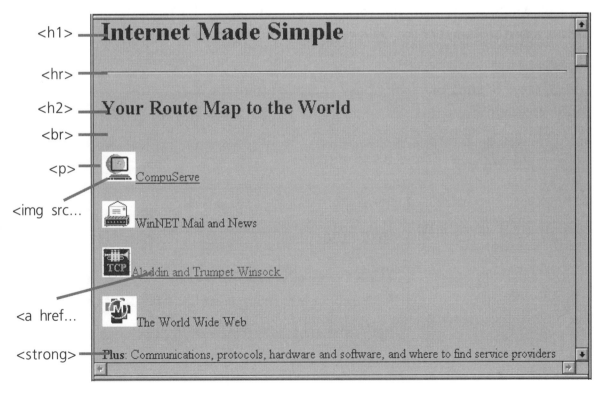

Major ftp sites

ftp.demon.co.uk (Demon Internet)

An excellent source of net tools and information – and while you're there you might look at what they have to offer as a service provider.

ftp.eff.org
The Electronic Frontier Foundation archives.

ftp.uwp.edu

Its /pub/msdos/games directory is a major store of games – and it is frequently so crowded you can't get in.

ftp.microsoft.com

Microsoft's ftp base. Search it for information and software they have released into the public domain.

micros.hensa.ac.uk

Lots of Windows stuff in /mirrors/cica/win3/desktop. This is a mirror (copy) of the main cica site in the States.

src.doc.ic.ac.uk (Sunsite UK)

– huge range of stuff, but a very busy site. Start from the /pub directory.

software.watson.ibm.com

IBM's public ftp site.

Tip

Pick your time carefully and you can download files faster. Avoid 7-11 in the evening, when you will be sharing your service provider's bandwidth with many other users. Avoid the working day at the ftp site, when you will be competing for the host computer's time with its local users.

Take note

This is a very limited selection of a huge number of sites, with the focus on those in or closest to the UK. A full list can be found at:

ftp://scitsc.wlv.ac.uk/pub/netinfo/ftpsites

9 Files by mail

Archie by mail 126

ftp by mail 128

Binaries by mail 130

Gopher by mail 132

Summary 134

Archie by mail

If you do not have an interactive connection to the Internet, you can run archie searches by mail. It may take up to a day for the results to get back to you, but at least you don't have to wait on-line while archie does its stuff.

- The mail should be addressed to:

  archie@*archie_server*

  where *archie_server* is any one of the servers listed on page 143. Example:

  archie@archie.doc.ic.ac.uk

- Anything in the **Subject** line is taken as part of the message, so it's simplest to leave this blank.

- Commands must start in the first column – leading tabs or spaces will kill a command line.

- To search for a file, use the command:

  find *filename*

  filename can be the whole name or a substring, as with interactive archie (page 102). Examples:

  find uuencode.com
  Specifies a particular encoding program.

  find ftp
  Guessing at the name of an ftp-handling program.

- If you give the whole filename, you can make it search for exact matches only by adding the command:

  search exact
  This doesn't just speed up the search, it also avoids having your returned mail clogged up with details of irrelevant files.

Tip

To get more detailed help on archie by mail, send a message containing the single word 'help' to an archie server.

Sample return mail from an archie search. There may be dozens of copies of the same file scattered over the Internet. This search turned up 14 files, including duplicates in different directories at the same site.

```
>> find uuencode.com
# Search type: sub.

Host nic.switch.ch    (130.59.10.40)
Last updated 04:13 25 Oct 1994

    Location: /mirror/msdos/starter
      FILE   -rw-rw-r--    997 bytes  11:07  5 Oct 1994  uuencode.com


Host micros.hensa.ac.uk    (148.88.8.84)
Last updated 03:30 29 Oct 1994

    Location: /mirrors/simtel/msdos/starter
      FILE   -r--r--r--    997 bytes  09:07  5 Oct 1994  uuencode.com


Host src.doc.ic.ac.uk    (146.169.43.1)
Last updated 08:30 31 Oct 1994

    Location: /computing/systems/ibmpc/simtel/starter
      FILE   -r--r--r--    964 bytes  09:07  5 Oct 1994  uuencode.com.Z
    ...
    ...
Host nic.switch.ch    (130.59.10.40)
Last updated 04:13 25 Oct 1994

    Location: /software/msdos/starter
      FILE   -rw-rw-r--    987 bytes  01:00 14 Mar 1991  uuencode.com
```

lines deleted

Filename

This is a file, not a sub-directory

Read/Write permissions, i.e. who can do what to the file. As long as it ends **r--**, you can get a copy of the file.

Size – useful to know before ftp-ing

Date – get the latest version

compressed by Unix – needs gnuzip or similar

ftp by mail

Having run archie by mail to track down the host, directory and name of a file, you can do ftp by mail to download it. This is not as convenient as interactive ftp, but it is a feasible way of getting files if you only have a mail connection. The commands are simple enough – the problems arise from the nature of the mail systems.

Mail is designed for text messages, so binary files have to be suitably encoded for mailing, then decoded on receipt (see page 130.) There is also a 100k limit to the size of files that can be handled by the mail systems, so large files have to be broken up into manageable chunks before sending – then reassembled afterwards.

ftp-by-mail requests should be addressed to the request handler at your service provider, or to:

> ftpmail@gatekeeper.dec.com

Example 1: A simple request for a directory listing:

> connect ftp.ibmpcug.co.
> cd /pub/WinNET
> ascii
> dir

Example 2: Getting MPEGWIN.ZIP, the MPEG video viewer:

> connect gatekeeper.dec.com
> cd /pub/micro/msdos/win3/desktop
> uuencode
> binary
> chunksize 100000
> get mpegwin.zip
> quit

This will come through in 8 bits, and must be patched back together before decoding. See page 131.

ftp commands

connect *hostname* – make the link to the remote system

cd or **chdir** *dirname* – change directory

uuencode – convert binary files to text

binary – switch to binary mode

chunksize *bytes* – size to chop large files into

ascii – switch to ascii text mode

dir – send a listing of the current directory

get *filename* – send the selected file

quit – close the connection

Tip

Stick to text files and smaller binary files at first - they give few problems.

```
REPLY-TO: ftpmail@ibmpcug.co.uk


total 1131
dr-xr-xr-x  2 root    daemon       224  Aug  3 11:30    COMPRESS
dr-xr-xr-x  2 root    daemon        32  May 26 17:23    FILES
dr-xr-xr-x  2 root    daemon        64  Aug 15 16:13    MAG
-r—r—r—   1 root    daemon      2934  Sep 13 14:26    README.NOW
dr-xr-xr-x  2 root    daemon       256  Sep  9 14:03    UTILS
dr-xr-xr-x  2 root    daemon        48  Jun 14 14:10    UUCP
-r—r—r—   1 root    daemon     12826  Sep 13 14:24    WinNET.txt
-r—r—r—   1 root    daemon     26400  Jun 20 11:07    internet.doc
-rw-r—r—  1 root    daemon     15561  Sep 12 11:55    internet.txt
-r—r—r—   1 root    daemon    202574  Oct  7 1993     pkz204g.exe
lrwxrwxrwx 1 root    daemon        10  May 27 13:42    readme -> README.NOW
-r—r—r—   1 root    daemon     10970  Aug 16 12:12    services
-r—r—r—   1 root    daemon     31824  Oct  6 1993     uudecode.exe
dr-xr-xr-x  2 root    daemon        80  Apr 13 12:28    v204
dr-xr-xr-x  2 root    daemon        48  Jun 15 13:04    win
lrwxrwxrwx 1 root    daemon        10  May 26 17:35    wn_news0.txt -> WinNET.txt
-r—r—r—   1 root    daemon    241211  Aug 11 15:23    wn_news1.zip
-r—r—r—   1 root    daemon    295408  Aug 11 15:23    wn_news2.zip
-r—r—r—   1 root    daemon    181866  Aug 11 15:23    wn_news3.zip
lrwxrwxrwx 1 root    daemon        12  Aug 12 15:37    wn_news4.zip ->
wn_tools.zip
-r—r—r—   1 root    daemon    396214  Sep 13 12:00    wn_tools.zip
-r—r—r—   1 root    daemon    723693  Aug 11 15:23    wnmail22.zip
-r—r—r—   1 root    daemon      7662  Sep  3 18:42    wnmsgate.txt
-r—r—r—   1 root    daemon     70554  Sep  3 22:22    wnmsgate.zip
-r—r—r—   1 root    daemon     80553  Sep 13 12:00    wntools.zip
```

Mail returned from a dir request .

The characters in the leftmost column are:

d = directory – add its name to the directory path and **dir** again to see what's in it

l = link to another file – ignore these

- = text or binary file – you can **get** these; **ascii** if they end in *.txt*, otherwise **binary**

Take note

Requests to popular sites can take a while to be processed. I had to wait a week for one file!

Binaries by mail

E-mail is based on simple ASCII text, using only 7 data bits per character, the eighth bit being kept for parity checks. Binary files - pictures, programs and sounds – use all 8 bits of every byte. So how can you send binaries by mail? The answer lies in a very neat pair of programs, **uuencode** and **uudecode**. (*uu* stands for *U*nix to *U*nix, which is how mail travels on much of its journey.) They turn binary files to and from 7-bit ASCII text. If you join any newsgroups that circulate binary files, you will need uudecode, and encode if you intend to post files.

When you have downloaded the programs (from your service provider, or by ftp – see the previous page) move them into your DOS or Windows directory.

❏ **Encode and Out**

1 Go into MSDOS and change to the directory containing the file to be encoded.

2 Encode with the line:

uuencode *filename*

❏ This produces a new file, with the same name but .UUE as the extension. e.g.

uuencode smile.bmp

produces

smile.uue

3 This is a text file. If you want to edit it to add a message, do so – just don't alter anything between the *begin* and *end*.

4 Your mail system have a method of sending text files, or attaching them to a message. Use it.

5 Post the mail

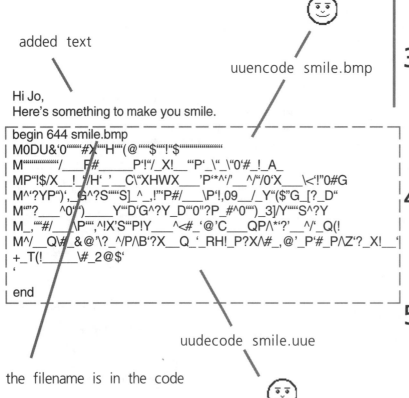

added text

uuencode smile.bmp

Hi Jo,
Here's something to make you smile.

```
begin 644 smile.bmp
M0DU&'0''""#X""H""(@"@"$"""$'$$$""""""""""""""""""
M""""""""//___P"#`#""""#P"|"/_/_X!""/""""""""
MP""#!!""#G|X."""0"""
M""""""
begin 644 smile.bmp
M0DU&'0'"#X"H"(@("o"@""$'$$$"""""""""""""""""""
M"""""""//___F"#"#""""P'I'/_/X!'%""P""""
MP"!$$X""!'H/H'"""""C
M^??[$\
end
```

the filename is in the code

uudecode smile.uue

Basic steps

Binaries and WinNET

□ In and Decode

1 Take your mail and either copy the section between *begin* and *end* into your editor, or copy in the whole message and chop off the surplus text.

2 Save the encoded part as a text file – the name is irelevant.

3 Go into MSDOS and change to the directory with the encoded file.

4 Decode with the line:

uudecode *filename*

□ This extracts the binary file, saving it with its original name.

WinNET mail has the encode/decode routines built into it, making the handling of binary files very simple.

When sending mail, there is an [Attach File] button in Quick Mail that leads to this dialog box. Just select the file to attach, and leave the rest to the system.

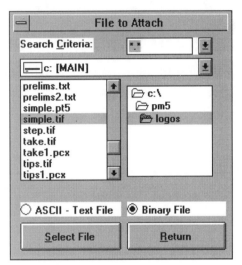

When receiving mail containing a binary, select the **Mail – Detach binary file** command, and give a filename. The system will cut out the *begin* to *end* part and decode it.

Take note

Mail messages and newsgroup articles are limited to 1000 lines. Large binary files may be split up over several mailings. Each part will be numbered and marked ---Cut here--- at the top and/or bottom. To decode these, you must cut out the encoded parts, stitch them back together in a text editor and save them as a single file. Run this through uudecode.

Gopher by mail

Perhaps the most intriguing thing about gophering by mail is that it is possible at all, but those of you who only have mail access to the Internet will be pleased to know that it can be done. However, patience is a virtue that you must possess for mail gophering. It can take a week to get to where you want to be.

The basic technique is simple. To start the process, send an e-mail to a gophermail server with the single message HELP. You will be sent back a menu. Mark an X by the side of any item that interest you and send it back. You will get another menu, or a document or whatever was pointed to by that item.

Use one of these gophermail sites:

gopher@dsv.su.se	(Sweden)
gophermail@calvin.edu	(USA)
gopher@earn.net	(USA)
gomail@ncc.go.jp	(Japan)

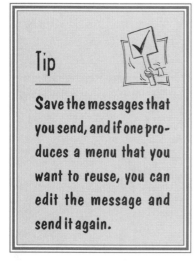

Tip

Save the messages that you send, and if one produces a menu that you want to reuse, you can edit the message and send it again.

1 Address an e-mail to a gophermail site, leaving the Subject blank and with the single word HELP as the message. Send it.

2 When the site writes back, check through the menu. If you see anything interesting, go into your editor to reply to it.

3 Place an X to the right of the desired item, and mail the message back.

4 Save the mail in case you want to reuse the menu – it will save having to go back to the start.

5 Repeat 2 to 4 until you find what you want.

REPLY-TO: gophermail@calvin.edu

Mail this file back to gopher with an X before the menu items that you want.
If you don't mark any items, gopher will send all of them.

  1. About The World Menu.
  2. All the Gopher Servers in the World (long list)/
  3. Europe/
  4. Michigan/
  5. Middle East/
  6. North America/
  7. Pacific/
  8. Research/
  9. South America/
 10. The Home of Gopher, University of Minnesota/
 11. The InfoSlug System, University of California - Santa Cruz/
 12. Various Internet Systems and Databases/
 13. Weather and More/
X 14. Wonderful Finds/
 15. Worldwide Internet Phone & Address Directories/

The / at the end indicates a menu.

No / so these must be documents

REPLY-TO: gophermail@calvin.edu
----

  1. ACADEME THIS WEEK (Chronicle of Higher Education)/
  2. About the Wonderful Finds Menu.
  3. Coalition for Networked Information (cni)/
  4. Computer Services/
  5. Government Information On-Line from eryx.syr.edu/
  6. MTV gopher (unofficial)/
  7. MedSearch America gopher/
  8. The Electronic Newsstand(tm)/
  9. The Internet Hunt/
 10. The Internet Mall.
 11. US State Department Travel Advisories/
 12. United Nations/

Tip

If you want to know more about mail access to ftp, gopher and other services, read Dr. Bob's (Bob Rankin) guide. To get your copy, send e-mail to:

MAILBASE @ mailbase.ac.uk Leave the Subject line blank, and enter this as the message: send lis-iis e-access-inet.txt

Summary

❑ **Archie, ftp, gopher** and other facilities can be used through the e-mail system, though it will typically take a day between sending a request and getting a reply.

❑ **Archie requests** can be done conveniently by e-mail – and you don't have to wait on-line while it archie searches.

❑ **Binary files** have to be endocded before they can be sent by mail, so you will need uudecode to restore them when you get them.

❑ When **large files** are broken into chunks before mailing, and will have to be reassembled in a text editor before decoding.

❑ If your mail system allows you to **attach binary files** to your messages, sending binaries becomes quite simple.

❑ You can **navigate gopherspace** by mail, but it is very slow.

10 Sources

UK service providers 136

Recommended ftps 140

Major ftp sites 142

Archie servers 143

Gopher servers 144

UK service providers

Mail and news services

If your main interest is communicating with others – either individually through e-mail or as a member of a newsgroup – consider one of these services. Remember that you still have access to the Internet's databases of files, using ftp by mail.

Direct Line Tel: 0181 845 8952

e-mail: sysop@ps.com

Nodes: London only

£25 per year. No time charges

On-line   Tel: 0181 558 6114

e-mail: jon@on-line.co.uk

Nodes: London and Dialplus (surcharge £1.60 p hour)

£10 per month or £2 per hour

Sound & Vision BBS E   Tel: 01932 253131

e-mail: info@span.com

Nodes: London and Surrey

£15 per year. No time charges

WinNET Mail & News Tel: 0181 863 1191

e-mail: request@win-uk.net (Subject: HELP)

Nodes: London, Cambridge, Edinburgh, Birmingham, Manchester, Bristol.

£6.75 per month

Off-line reading/writing only.

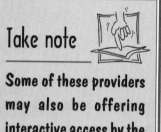

Take note

Some of these providers may also be offering interactive access by the time you read this. WinNET, as part of the PC User Group, already does.

Full Interactive Access

Aladdin   Tel: 01489 782221

e-mail: info@aladdin.co.uk

£25 registration/ software

£100 half-year,limit of 2 hours use during evenings

BBCNetworking Club Tel: 0181 576 7799

£25 sign up, £12 month

Home & educational users only

Cityscape Tel: 01223 566950

e-mail: sales@cityscape.co.uk

£25 sign up, £15 month Unlimited time

Sign up fee includes registered *shareware*

CIX Tel: 0181 296 9666

£30 sign up, £15 month for 20 hours

Also runs an extensive e-mail/newsgroups conferencing service

CompuServe Tel: 0800 289378

£6.20 per month (5 hours) + £1.95p.h.

Free software and trial offer - see page 60

Delphi Tel: 0171 757 7080

e-mail: ukservice@delphi.com

£10 month (4 hours) or £20/month (30 hours) + £3 p.h.

DemonInternet Tel: 0181 371 1234

e-mail: sales@demon.net

£12.50 registration £10 p. month.   No time charges.

The Direct Connection Tel: 0181 297 2200

e-mail: helpdesk@dircon.co.uk

£7.50 sign up £10 per month. No time charges

Dungeon Network Systems Tel: 01638 711 550

e-mail: info@dungeon.com

Nodes: East Anglia

£10 per month. No time charges.

Free Trial : Phone 01638 711 433;

Comms 8 data, None parity, 1 Stop bit;

login: guest no password

Easynet Ltd   Tel: 0171-209-0990

e-mail: admin@easynet.co.uk

Nodes: London

£25 registration/software. £9.90 per month.

GreenNet Tel: 0171 713-1941

e-mail: support@gn.apc.org

£5 per month + £3.60 per hour peak £2.40 off-peak

IBMNet   Tel: 0800 973000

£10 month (3hours) or £20 (30 hours) + £3 p.h.

Pavilion Internet Tel: 01273 607072

e-mail: info@pavilion.co.uk

Nodes: Sussex

£17.75 registration, £17.75 per month   No on-line charges.

Minimum subscription 6 months.

Pipex (Public IP Exchange Limited) Tel: 01223 250120

e-mail: sales@pipex.net

£50 sign up £180 p.a.

PC User Group (WinNET Mail & News) Tel: 0181 863 1191

e-mail: request@win-uk.net (Subject: HELP)

£6.75 per month (Off-line e-mail/news)

+ £8.25 per month Internet access

Free trial offer - see page 82

RedNet Tel: 01494 513 333

e-mail: info@rednet.co.uk

£25 registration/software, £15 per month no time charges

Total Connectivity Providers Tel: 01703 393392

e-mail: tcp@tcp.co.uk

£7 sign up £10 per month unlimited time

Free trial offer - see page 96

U-NET Limited   Tel: 01925 633144

e-mail: hi@u-net.com

Nodes: Lancashire

£12 registration, £12 per month

Take note

This list covers the larger service providers and some of the smaller ones with dial-in access throughout the UK.

The prices were correct at the end of 1995, but may well have changed – for the better. Increasing competition is pushing prices down.

Recommended ftps

General purpose tools

PKzip – standard compression/decompression utility:

ftp://kth.se/pub/tex/tools/pkzip/pkz204g.exe

WinZip – neat Windows version that Zips and Unzips (also handles files compressed by other programs):

ftp://sunsite.doc.ic.ac.uk/computing/systems/ibmpc/
windows3/util/winzip56.exe

uuencode – turns graphics and other binaries into text for sending through as mail or newsgroup articles:

ftp://micros.hensa.ac.uk/mirrors/simtel/msdos/starter/
uuencode.com

uudecode - turns uuencoded files back into binary form:

ftp://micros.hensa.ac.uk/mirrors/simtel/msdos/starter/
uudecode.com

Paint Shop Pro – excellent graphics conversionpackage, handling all the regularly used file formats. Can also be used for resizing, enhancing and manipulating images:

ftp://ftp.funet.fi/pub/msdos/windows/desktop/pspro20.zip

Winsock and Web tools

Trumpet Winsock – needed to handle a SLIP connection to the Internet, for Web browsing:

ftp://sunsite.doc.ic.ac.uk/computing/systems/ibmpc/
simtel/win3/winsock/twsk20b.zip

Netscape – Web browser:

ftp://ajk.tele.fi/PublicBinaries/msdos/winsock/ns16-
100.exe

Take note

The Internet is constantly changing. These URL's were correct at the time of writing, but may no longer be so. The version numbers are the most likely things to change – look out for similar filenames when you reach the host directories.

WSArchie – Winsock-client file locator

ftp://dorm.rutgers.edu/pub/msdos/winsock/apps/
    wsarchie.zip

ws_ftp – Winsock ftp software

ftp://dorm.rutgers.edu/pub/msdos/winsock/apps/
    ws_ftp.zip

hgopher – Winsock gopher software

ftp://dorm.rutgers.edu/pub/msdos/winsock/apps/
    hgopher2.3.zip

Eudora – Winsock e-mail software

ftp://ftp.qualcomm.com/windows/eudora/1.4/
    eudor144.exe

Reference materials

"There's Gold in them thar Networks", by Jerry Martin

ftp://bells.cs.ucl.ac.uk/rfc/rfc1402.txt

"Hitchhiker's Guide to the Internet", by Ed Krol

ftp://bells.cs.ucl.ac.uk/rfc/rfc1118.txt

.. and many more (not always that up-to-date) at

ftp://mailbase.ac.uk/internet-guides

Take note

Most of these are shareware. Try them for free, but if you are going to use them in earnest, do register. It rarely costs very much and it does help to keep the flow of shareware going.

Major ftp sites

ftp.demon.co.uk (Demon Internet)

Probably the best UK source of net tools and information.

ftp.eff.org

The Electronic Frontier Foundation archives.

ftp.uwp.edu

Its **/pub/msdos/games** directory is a major store of games
– and it is frequently so crowded you can't get in.

ftp.microsoft.com

Microsoft's ftp base. Search it for information and software they have released into the public domain.

micros.hensa.ac.uk

Lots of Windows stuff in **/mirrors/cica/win3/desktop**. This
is a mirror (copy) of the main cica site in the States.

src.doc.ic.ac.uk (Sunsite UK)

– huge range of stuff, but a very busy site. Start from the
/pub directory.

software.watson.ibm.com

IBM's public ftp site.

Take note

This is a very limited selection of a huge number of sites, with the
focus on those in or closest to the UK. A full list can be found at:

ftp://scitsc.wlv.ac.uk/pub/infomagic/internet.tools.cdrom/
msdos/wattcp/ftp.zip

Archie servers

Tip

At the time of writing, both the UK archie servers were often so busy that they were almost unusable. I find that archie.luth.se in Sweden usually gives the quickest responses.

United Kingdom
archie.doc.ic.ac.uk
archie.hensa.ac.uk
Europe

archie.switch.ch	Switzerland
archie.edvz.uni-linz.ac.at	Austria
archie.univie.ac.at	Austria
archie.funet.fi	Finland
archie.univ-rennes1.fr	France
archie.th-darmstadt.de	Germany
archie.rediris.es	Spain
archie.unipi.it	Italy
archie.luth.se	Sweden
archie.uninett.no	Norway
archie.ac.il	Israel

North America

archie.cs.mcgill.ca	Canada
archie.uqam.ca	Canada
archie.unl.edu	USA
archie.internic.net	USA
archie.rutgers.edu	USA
archie.ans.net	USA
archie.sura.net	USA

Far East

archie.wide.ad.jp	Japan
archie.hama.nm.kr	Korea
archie.sogang.ac.kr	Korea
archie.ncu.edu.tw	Taiwan
archie.au	Australia

Gopher servers

Some UK gopher servers

gopher.aston.ac.uk	(Aston University)
gopher.cranfield.ac.uk	(Cranfield Instute of Technology)
gopher.dmu.ac.uk	(De Montfort University)
gopher.ic.ac.uk	(Imperial College, London)
gopher.liv.ac.uk	(Liverpool University)
gopher.qmw.ac.uk	(Queen Mary & Westfield College)
gopher.bham.ac.uk	(Birmingham University)
gopher.brad.ac.uk	(Bradford University)
gopher.cam.ac.uk	(Cambridge University)
gopher.bham.ac.uk	(Birmingham University)
gopher.ed.ac.uk	(Edinburgh University)
gopher.newcastle.ac.uk	(Newcastle University)
gopher.nottingham.ac.uk	(Nottingham University)
gopher.wlv.ac.uk	(WolverhamptonUniversity)

Gopher mail servers

gopher@ftp.technion.ac.il	(Italy)
gopher@dsv.su.se	(Sweden)
gophermail@calvin.edu	(USA)
gopher@earn.net	(USA)
gopher@solaris.ims.ac	(USA)
gopher@join.ad.jp	(Japan)
gopher@nips.ac.jp	(Japan)
gomail@ncc.go.jp	(Japan)
gopher@nig.ac.jp	(Japan)

Tip

To find more Gopher servers, look for the Full list of Gophers around the world — it should be on the top level of your home gopher menu.

Index

A

Addresses, e-mail 9

Addressing systems 8

Almac 39

Anonymous ftp 18

ANSI terminal emulation 38

ANSI.SYS 39

Archie 20, 102

Archie, by mail 126

Article, in newsgroups 14

Ascii 34

AT command set, modems 42

Auto Load Images, Netscape 114

B

BABT approval 33

Bandwidth 16

Baud rate 31

BBC URL 118

Binary file transfers, Terminal 56

Binary files 35

Binary files, by mail 130

Binary files, reassembling 131

Binary files, via WinNET 131

Bookmarks, gopher 107

Bookmarks, Netscape 120

C

Call Server, WinNET 88

Carrier 43

CCITT 31

Chat lines 26

Checksum 36

CIM 64

COM ports 33

Comit comms software 40

Communications, CompuServe 78

Communications Software 40

Compuserve Information Manager,
    downloading 64

CompuServe, joining 62

Computer, suitable for comms 30

Conference areas, CompuServe 72

Connector, Terminal 49

CPU utilization, WInNET 87

CRC 36

Cyclical Redundancy Check 36

D

Data bits 35

Data Communications Equipment 43

Data compression 32

Data Terminal Equipment 43

Data Terminal Ready, modem signal 43

Data transfer protocols 36

DCE 43

Dial-up, automatic, WinNET 91

Dial-up Unix connections 89

Directories of the Web 116

Domains 8

DOS-based comms software 40

Downloading 18

Downloading binary files, Terminal 56

Downloading, ftp 105

DTE 43

DTR 43

E

E-mail 12

E-mail addresses 9

E-mail, CompuServe 78

E-mail, through Winsock 108

E-mail, WinNET 88

Echo 38

Electronic mail 12

Error detection 34

Eudora 108

Even parity 34

F

FAQ 2

File finder, CompuServe 74

File transfer 18

File Transfer Protocol 18

File transfers, ftp 105

Files, finding 20, 126

Files, finding with archie 102

Finding files 20

Flame 16

Forums 72

Frequently Asked Questions 2

ftp 18

ftp, by mail 128

ftp, through CompuServe 76

ftp, through Winsock 104

ftp, via Netscape 112

G

Games 26

GIF file type 57

GIF graphic format 112

Gigabyte 4

GO facility, CompuServe 68

Gopher 24

Gopher, by mail 132

Gopher Jewels 24

Gopher, through Winsock 106

Gopher, via Netscape 112

Gopherspace 24

H

Handshaking 37

Hard disk space, disappearing fast 95

Hardware handshaking 37

Hayes-compatible modems 33

Help, Netscape 114

Helper Applications, Netscape 115

HGOPHER 106

HTML 22, 122

Hypertext 22

HyperText Markup Language 122

I

Interactive connection 18

Interactive services 26

Interesting Devices 117

Internet, size estimates 6
Internet Society 2
IP address 99
IRQ settings 33

J

JIF file type 57
JPEG graphic format 112
JPG file type 57

K

Kermit 36

L

LAN 2
Libraries, CompuServe 72
Local Area Network 2
Local Echo 50
Local links 98
Local nodes, CompuServe 68
Log on 12
Login script, WInsock 100
Lurk 16

M

Microcom Network Protocol 32
MNP 32
Modem 31
Modem commands 42
Modem Commands, Terminal 51
Mosaic 22
MPEG files 102

MUD 26
MUD, demo 101

N

Naming conventions 8
Net Directories 116
Netiquette 16
Netscape 112
Netscape Help 114
Netscape options 114
Network configuration, Eudora 108
Newsgroup subscription 92
Newsgroups 14
Newsgroups, via Netscape 112

O

Odd parity 35
Off-line mail, WinNET 88
Off-line reader 12
Off-line mail, WinNET 88
Off-line work, CompuServe 70

P

Packet mode enabled, Winsock 101
Parallel port 32
Parity 34
PC User Group 84
Phone commands, Terminal 46
Phone menu, Terminal 59
Point-Of-Presence 109
POP accounts 109
Port 32

Post 14
Preferences, CompuServe 67
Preferences, Terminal 50
Protocols 34, 36
Pulse dialing 51

R

Receive Text File.. Terminal 53
Remote Host, ftp 104
RLE file type 57

S

Scheduler, WinNET 91
Serial port 32
Service Providers 2
Settings, Terminal 48
Setup string, modem 42
SLIP 22
SLIP port 99
Smiley 17
Snail mail 12
Star Trek 95
Stop bits 35
Subscribing, newsgroups 92

T

TCP 99
TCP Error message 112
TCP/IP 22
Telephone connection 30
TeleTYpe 38
Telnet 20

Terminal emulation 38
Terminal Emulation, Windows Terminal 50
Terminal screen 46
Terminal, Windows program 40, 46
Text capture 52
Text files, sending 54
Text Transfers, Terminal 52
TIA 118
TIF file type 57
Timeout limits 48
Tone dial 51
Transfer Control Protocol 99
Transmission speeds 31
Trumpet Winsock 99
TTY 38

U

Uniform Resource Locator 9
Uploading 18
Uploading, ftp 105
URL 9
URL, for ftp 18
URL, World Wide Web 22
URLs, ftp 104
URL's, World Wide Web 118
USENET newsgroups 14
UUCICO 89
uudecode 130
uuencode 130

V

V numbers, modems 31

V.42bis data compression 32

Veronica 24

Viewers, in Gopher 106

Viewers, Netscape 115

VT-100 terminal 38

VT-52 terminal 38

W

WAIS 25

WAN 2

Web browser 22

Web pages, creating 122

Whole Internet Catalog 116

Wide Area Network 2

WinCIM 64

WinCIM screen 70

Windows 95 30

WinNET, joining 84

WinNET Mail and Tools, downloading 84

WinNET tools 90

Winsock 99

Word Wrap, Terminal 54

Works 40

World Wide Web 22

WS_FTP 104

WSARCHIE 103

X

Xmodem 36

Xmodem, in Terminal 56

XON/XOFF handshaking 37

Y

Yahoo Web directory 117

Ymodem 36

Z

ZIP files 32

Zmodem 36

Zones 8

Also available from Butterworth Heinemann...

After you've read The Internet Made Simple, here's the next book you should buy; become a whiz on the Internet with...

THE INTERNET WITH WINDOWS – Glyn Moody

- 650 pages
- £19.99
- More than 1000 Internet addresses in Europe, the US and Asia for you to visit
- Over 500 Windows 95 screen shots
- Full glossary
- Can be used by both Windows 3.1 and Windows 95 users

This book:

- Gives simple-to-understand explanations of all the basic Internet concepts, with many practical examples
- Provides a comprehensive guide to accessing 99% of the Internet's resources with just electronic mail
- Gives step-by-step instructions on how to set up the Internet programs contained in Windows 95 and Windows Plus!, and how to obtain and set up equivalent software for Windows 3.1 (which can also be used with Windows 95)
- Explains how to obtain and configure most of the hundred or so Windows Internet shareware programs that are currently available, with detailed tips for using them. These include software for all the main tools – e-mail, Usenet, FTP, telnet, Archie, Gopher, WAIS and the World-Wide Web (WWW) – as well as more unusual ones such as Ping, TraceRoute, Finger, Host Lookup, X.500, Whois, Ph, Chat, IRC, Internet programs that use Virtual Reality, and others that enable you to carry on international conversations for the price of a local call.
- Gives simple instructions on how to set up the leading WWW programs Netscape and Mosaic and includes step-by-step details of how to write your own Web home page using just a text editor
- Tells you how to find things and people on the Internet, with explicit information about search tools and practical examples
- Contains over one thousand interesting Internet addresses to visit, organised in a natural and easy-to-find way, complete with a unique index

Glyn Moody has been writing about computers and communications for fifteen years. His highly-popular Getting Wired page about the Internet appears every Thursday in Computer Weekly, and he also writes for The Guardian, The Daily Telegraph and specialist titles.

246x189mm   1996 isbn: 0 7506 2099 4   £19.99   paperback 650pages